BETTER THAN NOTHING

A Nurse and an Indigenous Community in the Australian Outback

By Philomena
with Marjorie MacKinnon

Incognito Publishing
Queensland, Australia
Incognitopublishing.au@gmail.com

First published May 2024

Copyright © 2024

ISBN: 978-0-6459691-0-8 (paperback)
       978-0-6459691-1-5 (ebook)

Subjects: Non-fiction/memoir/ Medicine and Nursing/Indigenous
Peoples/Racism and Discrimination/Social Justice/ Western Australia

A catalogue record for this
work is available from the
National Library of Australia

CONTENTS

Foreword... vii

PART 1: From Nepal to the Outback 1

From Marble Bar to Nullagine.................................... 10

    Knifing... 14

PART 2: Life in the Outback 19

Contact Tracing.. 19

Early Days.. 21

Indigenous Names... 22

    Nabaroo... 23

Beyond the Call of Duty 24

Stumpy and the Dead Women...................................... 29

The Snake Pit.. 32

Dinner Date.. 35

Alone with a Murderer.. 39

Useful Snakes... 41

The Burial of Eve's Baby.. 44

Jimmy: An Old Goldminer.. 47

New Policeman in Town... 49

Samuel and the Postal Service 52

The Boys Not Taken 53

Outback Accident.. 54

Reporting In... 56

Unusual Flowers 58

Helen's Injured Legs... 59

Chased... 62

Lore... 65

    Rite of Passage.. 65

Tribal Justice... 66

Trina's Rape.. 68

Cars in the Outback 70

The Satellite Dish.. 72

Encounters with Paedophilia........................ 75

Evan and Outback Politics............................ 79

The Canadian Miner in Trouble..................... 81

How The Desert People Lived 85

    Time and Money.................................... 86

    How They Cook.................................... 86

    The Stars Above.................................... 87

    Sex Education....................................... 87

    Walkabouts 88

    Keeping Cool.. 88

    Long Time No See................................ 89

    Help Yourself....................................... 90

Jason and Cathy... 91

Daphanie and Classroom Discipline 94

Sergeant B Stories 95

    Paddy Wagon Terror 96

    Friday Night at the Pub......................... 97

    Over My Dead Body............................. 97

Trina and the Christian Revival..................... 98

Down in the Pits 103

The Lebanese Doctor.................................. 106

Stolen Children Reunion 107

Swabs Were Not Enough............................. 111

Bush Medicine.. 112

Skinned Alive 115

Cemetery Cleanup 117

Nearly Choked to Death.............................. 120

Olive: "I Blind Bugger"............................... 123

Suicide Prevention... 125
Nabaroo: He Too Far Gone! 126
Rock Concert... 131
Mistaken Identity.. 133
Indigenous Funerals.. 136
Tobias and the Good Copper 141
Isabel in Labour... 143
Pub Apartheid... 146
Newman Morgue.. 153
Treatment for Depression................................... 156
Eve in Custody... 159
It's Important!... 162
Things to Know.. 164
Tragedy.. 167
Hot Tar Treatment.. 170
Picking up the Pieces... 172
Violence and Aboriginal Women........................ 173
The Blackfella Doctor 176
The Love of Samuel and Helen........................... 179
Under Surveillance... 180
Astral Travel.. 182
Trina's Dead Baby.. 185
Staying Alive 187
A Personal Thanks to the RFDS......................... 190
Breakthrough... 193
Invitation to a Corroboree 195

Epilogue... 197
Acknowledgements 199
Suggested Readings.. 200
About the Authors.. 201

INDIAN
OCEAN

Broome •

Port
Hedland
Karratha •
• Roebourne
North
West Cape
Exmouth •

GREAT SANDY
DESERT

Marble •
Bar

• Nullagine

Paraburdoo •
Newman •

GIBSON DESERT

Jigalong •

Carnarvon •

WESTERN
AUSTRALIA

LITTLE SANDY
DESERT

Denham

Wiluna •
Meekatharra •

Kalbarri •

Mount
Magnet •

Geraldton •

Leonora •

Dongara •

Kalgoorlie •

Northam •
Merredin •
Perth •

Norseman •

Foreword

Philomena has no desire for fame or fortune. For this reason, she has prohibited me from disclosing her full name and many personal details. She is elderly now, but as stubborn as the day she was born. In fact, it took two years of pulling teeth and Job-like patience to extract the stories contained in this book. It was worth it. Philomena's recollections merit our attention if we are to attain a more just society within Australia.

For fifteen incredible years, Philomena ("Philla") served as a remote-area community nurse in the Outback of Western Australia. She was stationed in Nullagine, a tiny mining town that is also the place of the Yirrangadji Indigenous Community. The Martu make up the bulk of its tiny population. Although this portion of Philomena's life took place between 1981 and 1996, her experiences and recollections are relevant as ever. If we look at the statistics, we can see that not much has changed.

The "town" (if you can call it that) was in spinifex country, sandy and blazing hot like the famous Gibson and Sandy Deserts. There was a pub, petrol station, grocery store, police station/jail, two-room school and her medical clinic. Like the police, she was provided with a modest house, which meant that she was on call 24/7.

When Philomena first arrived in the Pilbara, living conditions on the reserve were primeval. Indigenous people lived in humpies. Under normal conditions, inhabitants would bathe in the nearby river but there had been several years of drought. Locals were dirty, coated in the local red dust. Children wore rags and had lice. School attendance wasn't a priority. Drinking was. Many children were neglected, some women were violently abused, and communicable diseases like scabies and syphilis were prevalent.

The nearest hospital was in Port Hedland, which was about 325 kilometres away on corrugated roads. The Royal Flying Doctor Service flew into Nullagine once a fortnight, and they responded to emergency call-outs. Serious cases were often transported 1364 kilometres to the Royal Perth Hospital.

Once a week fresh fruit and vegetables would arrive, but they usually sold out within a couple of hours. Any major grocery shopping took place in Newman, which was almost a 200-kilometre drive each way. Nothing was easy.

In Nullagine, Philomena was truly on her own - the only medical practitioner for more than a hundred kilometres. "There were so many times I didn't know what to do," she explained. "I had no support. I couldn't contact [reach] anyone." It wasn't like a hospital setting where there were doctors and surgeons on hand, medical equipment, medicines, and security. As Stephen Langford noted in his book about the Royal Flying Doctors, remote nurses even drove their own ambulances.

Philomena felt overwhelmed and ill-equipped for such

a daunting mission. But then she realised that without her, this Indigenous community would have *nothing*. At least she was better than nothing! Over time, she discovered that Indigenous people were often treated like nothing, not only by non-Indigenous but, at times, by one another. Hence, the title of this book is meant to reflect this double meaning.

This collection of stories was more than 12 years in the making. The last two years we pushed and persisted out of a strong desire to bring attention to the vulnerability of under-educated Indigenous people, to the failings of legislation, and to the "cracks in the system", which enable exploitation, inadequate services and abuse of power. At times the language might appear antiquated; however, our intention is to stay true to the spirit of the times. No offence is intended.

Philomena's experiences provide valuable insights into the lives and treatment of Western Australia's Indigenous Desert People. Some of her stories are sweet, some are funny, but many are heartrending. We must read her book in its entirety in order to see this world through her eyes. In doing so, we are drawn into this community and leave with a deeper understanding of Indigenous people whose voices have yet to be heard.

Marjorie MacKinnon

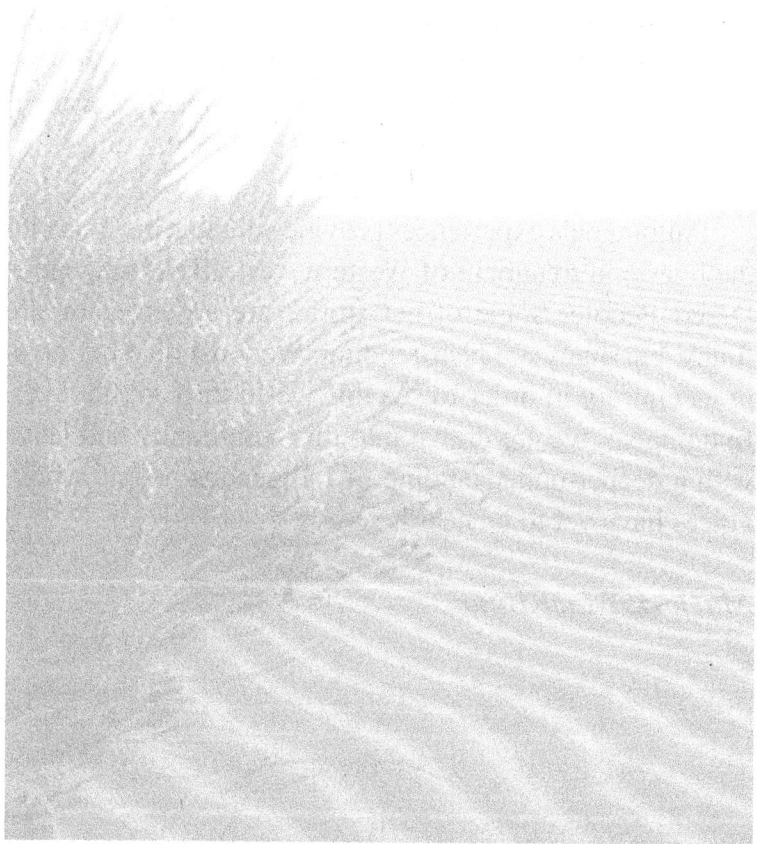

A memoir

Western Australia

1981-1996

PART 1

From Nepal to the Outback

In 1981 I was days away from going to work with Mother Theresa of Calcutta when the phone rang at my home in Mossman, Sydney.

"Linda here. I am going to Nepal on Friday. I rang to say goodbye." Linda and I had met while completing a midwifery course a few months before.

I quickly responded, "May I go with you? I am due to fly to Calcutta on Sunday. I could change the date and direction." This was an opportunity I didn't want to miss. Kathmandu! The Himalayas! This was more appealing than going to Calcutta. I had been there previously for three months and I knew what I was in for. I would have to find my own accommodation and support myself financially while I worked.

"Yes, come. I will meet you at Mascot Airport. Flight QF375. If you are not there, I will know you couldn't change your tickets."

I had no difficulty with the airline. I knew an American, called Mitch, who was working in Kathmandu and he offered accommodation for the two of us on arrival. The first night in Kathmandu, Mitch advised us to do the Buddhist retreat for a month because it had made a great impression on him when he did it. Off we went for a three-hour bus trip. Then a solid hour's walk into the foothills of the Himalayas. The cost was $100 USD for bed, lodging, *and* Buddhist teachings for the entire month's stay!

There were about ninety people from all walks of life. We ate once a day, meditated seven to nine hours a day, and received instruction on Buddhist philosophy. I stayed an additional six weeks to study Tibetan medicine. It was a once-in-a-lifetime opportunity. Moreover, it would be a wonderful adjunct to my nursing experience in geriatrics, psychiatry, maternity, and general medicine.

My epiphany came when the Buddhist Lama told us, "Help your own people. Help your own country. If you were born an Anglican, be very good at that. That is how you are true to Self. You work for your own country."

That lecture impressed all of us. My decision was made: Return to Australia. Forget Calcutta and Mother Theresa. Who were the poorest and most neglected in Australia? Answer: Our Aboriginals! So, I decided to go and work with our Indigenous people.

Returning home, I went to Centrelink in Sydney where I saw a nursing job advertised for the Outback in Western Australia. A nurse was needed to help two other nurses posted there. For a week I tried to make contact with the number on the ad, but their only reply was, 'We're interested and we'll get back to you'. After three such phone calls, I decided to catch a train to Perth and sort matters out more efficiently. I was *determined* to do this!

In Perth I stayed with one of my cousins who lived in the suburbs. The next morning, I caught a bus into town and looked for the Health Department. As fate would have it, I went into the wrong building, the Community Health Department. They were not hiring for the Kimberly, but said they were 'desperate' for someone in the Outback. I never heard of the location so I asked (naively), "Are there any Aborigines there?"

The nurses burst out laughing. "That's certainly blackfella country, if that's what you want! Have you ever heard of Marble Bar?"

I replied, "Yes, that's the hottest place in Australia."

"Well, that's where we want you to go. Are you still interested?"

"Yes, I suppose so. When do I go?"

I completed a requisite six-week training course for remote-area nursing. Surgical procedures, immunizations, sexually transmitted diseases, eye health, ear health, dealing with fractures, and general nursing skills were learned and practised. On the final day, we were briefed about Aboriginal culture. The speaker was an Indigenous woman who was probably recruited from the secretarial pool. She was only with us for one hour (out of six weeks!) but we were captivated and hungered for more.

Once my course was completed, I was given a one-way plane ticket to Port Hedland. I was assured there was no need for phone numbers or addresses because someone would be at the airport to meet me. So, at 5:30am I departed Perth. When I arrived in Port Hedland two hours later, there was no one there to meet me! All the other passengers got in cars and left. I was alone, totally alone. Just then I noticed a taxi that was about to leave and I called out to him. He too was surprised that nobody was meeting me. When I asked him to take me to the Health Department, he assured me he knew where it was. Well, he didn't. We landed at the Social Services Department. And it was closed. I realised this was the wrong address and I told him to take me to the Health Department.

When I ended up at the Port Hedland Hospital, nobody knew what I was talking about. No one was hiring nurses. When I explained that I was going to work at Marble Bar, they said, "You want Community Health," and they directed me to another building that was not nearby. I dragged my suitcase down steep, rough stairs and found a side door and I banged on it.

"Nobody uses this door," a voice called out. "Go around the front."

When I finally found the entrance I said, "I'm the nurse for Marble Bar."

I was greeted with questions like, "How did you get here?" and "Where did you come from?" They explained that this was the first time that no one was at the airport to greet people from the Department. Just my luck.

The following day, a Port Hedland nurse, whom I'll call Belinda, was appointed to drive me (nearly 650 kilometres) to Marble Bar and Nullagine and then back to Port Hedland for a one-day orientation. We were also expected to bring back a second vehicle, a four-wheel drive truck, from Nullagine that would be for my use in the Outback. When we reached the far side of Marble Bar, Belinda stopped the car and pointed to a small duplex and said that was where I would be living. There wasn't time to go in and look at it. "There's nothing to look at anyhow," she explained.

From there we turned back to town, which was small, but tidy. I could see a hotel and a store with one petrol bowser. Nearby was the new Community Health Centre, where I would be working. It was a transportable building that consisted of a one-room office with a sink and an adjoining toilet. This was run by a recently appointed Indigenous woman, Betty, who served as a liaison with the local community. Betty showed us the Aboriginal camps and introduced us to some of the people. From there we drove to the Nursing Post and met a registered nurse and her husband. Their home and the Nursing Post were adjoined and air-conditioned. It was blazing hot so an air-conditioner was more valuable than gold!

This office was located at the top of a steep hill so part of my job was to transport people to their clinic. Later we drove by an impressive Court House where the police had their offices and the Mines Registry was located. During the gold rush days, Marble Bar had a population of over five thousand people. Now there were fewer than four hundred. Great facilities for such a remote outpost.

After eating lunch in the car, we drove onward about 120 kilometres to Nullagine where we met a nurse stationed there. This wasn't an easy drive. Roads were unsealed and corrugated. It was slow going. When we got to Nullagine, I could only see a handful of buildings, including a simple house that served as the Nursing Post. The nurse stationed there was pregnant. She and Belinda seemed to know each other and enjoyed talking together. I didn't pay much attention to their conversation because I was busy looking over the clinic. Then I stepped outside and was bedazzled by the landscape. Coming from Sydney where buildings block your view, it was mesmerizing to see the vast, colourful nothingness that stretched as far as the eye could see.

Time was ticking by, and I was becoming increasingly anxious because daylight would soon slip away. I didn't really know the way back to Port Hedland and the dirt roads linked with many *unmarked* clay side roads. As importantly, cattle roamed freely and the potential for an accident was greater if we drove in the dark.

The nurse suggested I take her sedan (rather than the 4WD that I was assigned) and she would follow me in about 10 minutes. I wasn't sure I could find the way back, but Belinda assured me she would be right behind me. It was already twilight when I headed from Nullagine to Port Hedland. Night fell like a black, velvet curtain. It was hard to see the dirt road because it blended into the desert. I drove slowly to avoid hitting kangaroos and scrub bulls (cattle) that could be standing in the middle of the road.

There were no fences, no signs, no road lines. Within an hour my car slowly came to a complete stop!

At first, I thought I wasn't pushing hard enough on the accelerator, but no. I checked the petrol gauge and it was fine. I rolled down the windows but was immediately besieged by an army of insects (large grasshoppers, horse flies, moths, etc.) that whacked me on my head, with several staying in my hair and crawling across my scalp. Ugh!! I immediately turned off the headlights and got out of the car so that I could shake the bugs out of my hair. It was then that I realised just how deadly silent and dark it was. Pure blackness. I reassured myself that Belinda would soon arrive because I had driven so slowly. No one came. Eventually, I felt my way to the back of the car and opened the boot. I found a tyre iron and took it for protection. Bear in mind that I had just arrived from the Eastern States where girls went missing and were never heard of again.

Finally! I could hear a road train approaching in the distance but I could not see any lights. It took almost 10 minutes before I saw his headlights and it was another 15 minutes before he arrived. That's how dark and still it was in the desert. I put my headlights on and stood in front of my car and held my arms in the air. The driver came to a stop about 50 metres from me. I could see him getting something out of his cabin. What was he doing? Then, he got out of the truck and walked towards me. It appeared to me that he was hiding something behind his back. I was scared. Where was that bloody nurse?

The lights from our vehicles lit the road between us like a stage. I could only see his silhouette. As he got closer, he suddenly held out his arm and said, "You must really need a drink!" and he handed me a very cold can of Coke Cola. I breathed a sigh of relief, gratefully accepted the soda, and took a few mouthfuls immediately. I explained that there was a mechanical problem with my car. It just died.

"I'll go into town and send someone back for you," he offered.

"No way!" I reacted. "I'm not staying here in this pitch-black dark!"

He laughed at my fear and said, "You have to stay. Lady, they will steal all your tyres!"

"This is a Health Department car!" I shouted. There was *no way* I was going to remain alone in this wilderness just to guard some tyres!

"Oh, I understand. It's government property." He laughed. "Alright, you can come with me."

When we arrived at Nullagine, he let me off because he was continuing his journey to Perth. I thanked him and went into the pub. There I found that bloody nurse standing at the bar, drinking beer and eating hot chips with three young, strong, handsome miners standing around her. Bloody hell! I saw red.

Did she get a shock when she saw me? Yes, she did. But instead of apologising, Belinda barraged me with questions: "Why are you here? I sent you off to Port Hedland! Didn't you go? What have you been doing?"

"You were going to follow me!" I countered. "Where were *you*? The car broke down 60 k's out!"

"I don't believe you," she replied. "How did you get

back? How can you be here so quickly if the car broke down?" She sounded as angry as I did!

The audience of men started to laugh at us. One called out, "Get into it, girls!"

I was too angry to be deterred. I said to Belinda: "You're supposed to look after me! You're responsible for me! You left me sitting out there in the dark, on my own and you did *not* follow me!"

"I've only been here 20 minutes!" she insisted. "How could you get back so quickly? I find it hard to believe you." Clearly, she had lost track of time and was distracted by the cold beer, tasty chips and hot men.

"A truckie stopped and brought me here," I answered.

In a very shocked voice, she exclaimed, "You got in with a truckie!"

The men burst out laughing. It was commonly assumed that if a woman got a ride with a truckie she would repay with sexual favours. Ha-ha.

"We'll go straight away," the nurse conceded.

"I'm hungry. I've got to have something to eat," I insisted.

As a compromise, I ordered from the bar and ate my meal in *my* truck as we headed back to Port Hedland.

The following day, I had to prepare my Health Department vehicle. I gathered medical supplies and personal provisions (including sheets and towels) for my move to Marble Bar. I headed out at daybreak in case I got a puncture or my truck broke down. The drive was daunting. In Sydney I drove a small Honda, but now I had to get used to managing a 4WD truck that was big enough for two petrol tanks. I felt so alone and isolated. There were no vehicles on the road, no buildings, no people, and no animals in sight. The landscape was completely barren, yet stunningly beautiful. The royal blue sky contrasted with the red dusty soil and black-covered hills.

The drive went well, and I arrived at my humble half-duplex before noon. The biggest shock was the air-conditioner had not been turned on. Everything was so dry and the house was *roasting* hot. When I opened the kitchen tap, brown water sputtered out. And when I flushed the toilet, tiny brown frogs spun out! I plugged in the fridge, turned on the air-conditioner, and unloaded my provisions before going to the clinic to organise the medical supplies. And so began my life in the Western Australian Outback.

From Marble Bar to Nullagine

Bright and early on my first day I went down to the Community Health Clinic, which was located in a transportable building that was about the size of a shipping container. There I was greeted by Betty, the health worker whom I had met during my orientation. She wore a little blue dress and had her hair drawn back tightly. As we chatted, she helped me to understand the background to our situation.

The Nursing Post at the top of the hill was affiliated

with hospital services and was run by a qualified RN. She worked there and lived next door with her husband. She didn't go out into the community. The police used to do rounds in their patrol car every morning and take Indigenous patients up to the Nursing Post in their cruiser. Betty had been a cleaner at the clinic; then someone had the bright idea that doing follow-up, seeing people had their meds, doing preventions, and transporting patients were important as anything else.

Community nursing was a new position in Marble Bar. We were supposed to handle a lot of the little things ourselves. Many people in the Indigenous community slept and cooked outdoors in their camps. Their hygiene was poor so I tested and treated a number of communicable diseases, like hepatitis and sexually transmitted diseases. Often there were outbreaks of shigella (bacterial infection) where you pass "tomato soup" from your bowel. I took people's blood pressure, dressed wounds, provided postnatal care and conducted prevention programs, such as going to the school and giving vaccinations. Of course, everything had to be documented so there was endless paperwork as well.

Flies (the flies!) abounded in the Outback and they were a constant source of eye and ear problems. Specialists from Perth would come through a couple of times a year and they'd give us recommendations. For example, whenever the trachoma teams (founded by Dr Fred Hollows) came through, my role was to ensure that ongoing treatment continued for three weeks. This meant I would go down to the Aboriginal camps and just wash patients' eyes and apply eye drops each day. This was vital work because it could save people from going blind.

Another medical team from Perth focused on ear problems. Because of their rough living conditions, Indigenous children *especially* had dreadful problems. Their ears were so infected, they were overflowing with pus. I would use a syringe to pick out the flies that were lodged therein. I'm not kidding when I tell you I got 27 flies out of one child's ears (13 from the left, 14 from the right side)!

Betty's principal job was to drive patients up to the Nursing Post and to bring them back home afterwards. The hill was very steep and the temperature was extremely hot. Often patients were old and sick; they weren't able to walk back. Once a week, the Royal Flying Doctor Service (henceforth referred to as the RFDS), commonly known as the Flying Doctors, came to Marble Bar. On RFD days, Betty would drive the medics from the airstrip to the Nursing Post. We were also dependent on the Flying Doctors for bringing meds. Betty would bring the medications to the clinic and we would distribute them as directed.

We were "Community Health". That was my job, that's what I was hired for. My co-worker, Betty, and I were flat-out providing ongoing care. So, it was a big shock when a couple of days after arriving in Marble Bar, my boss, a Hedland nurse, rang me and said I was to go to Nullagine. The pregnant nurse who had been working there had left. It became my responsibility! She explained that the Flying

Doctors had rung up and said there were some people sick under the tree. I was to go there and make an assessment.

As I drove the 120 kilometres to Nullagine, I kept thinking, 'What am I going to *do*?' This was a whole other level of medical care! As I drove slowly into town, I could see a bunch of Aboriginals under the shade of a tree. They must have recognised the Health Department vehicle because they started jumping up and down, trying to get my attention. Several people waved their arms to beckon me towards them. As I got closer, they started making kissy faces! I soon realised that the Indigenous people do not use their fingers to point. They use their lips! They were signalling 'Look at them. They're the ones you got to look at'. When you're a nurse you get to know all these things.

"Is this the sick one?" I asked.

"Yair," was the reply. They didn't say yes and no.

I looked at the woman who was lying on the ground. She had pneumonia. "Ah, yes. She's really sick, isn't she?" I nodded.

There were a couple of other people needing treatment, including one with a broken arm. I tried to get these patients into my truck to transport them back to Marble Bar. But they kept saying, "No, no! Fix us here. Fix us here!"

"I can't!" I explained. "I got nothing! I've got no drugs. I got no water!" We argued a bit. But I came to appreciate that they were desert people. This was their country. They didn't want to go to a whitefella hospital.

Because they were so sick, somebody would have

given them beer to drink. At this point, they were almost in a stupor. The beer was their analgesic. "I'm not too bad," each patient insisted. Never mind they could die in another 24 hours!

As a compromise, they got in my truck and I drove them to the Nullagine clinic. I did a few things for them then drove them back to the tree. I didn't have a phone. Only a radio. I had been given a lesson, but I still wasn't very good at using it. I tried radioing my boss but I couldn't get through. So, I went to the police station and asked to use their phone.

When I spoke to the Hedland nurse, I advised her that the woman with pneumonia definitely needed to be hospitalised. I was told the Flying Doctors were doing a clinic somewhere else, and they could come to Nullagine around 2 o'clock to have a look at everyone. Was that alright? I said that was fine. When the time came, I drove the sick and injured to the airstrip. The RFDS took all four patients back with them. There was still enough daylight so I drove back home to Marble Bar.

Knifing

Not long after my call-out trip to Nullagine, I got a phone call around midnight from one of the Flying Doctors. He said, "You know it costs $600 to take the plane out."

"Y-e-s," I replied warily.

"The Nullagine police rang us. There's been a fight. We don't know if he's dead. They don't seem to be able to talk straight about it. Do you think you could go down and have a look at him?"

Not much time had passed since my car had broken down on that deserted clay road between Marble Bar and Nullagine. The memory of being stranded all alone in the dark was still fresh in my mind. No! No! I thought. However, in those days, funding for the RFDS was precarious and inadequate. They really had to watch every penny. I was the closest medical practitioner so I could see his point.

Despite my reluctance, I got in the truck and drove into the dead of night over those unmarked, corrugated roads to Nullagine. When I arrived, I discovered that a man had been stabbed, and the police didn't know whether to keep the knife in or to take it out. As they explained, "We've always been told, 'Don't pull out the knife,'" which was the standard advice. I phoned the Flying Doctor to report the situation.

"What do they think? Do they think the guy is going to live the rest of his life with a knife in him, do they?" the doctor groused. "Do they think he's going to walk around with a knife in him, and we're going to just give him some pills and he'll be all right?"

"They've got me so paranoid I thought I'd ring you before I pulled the knife out," I explained.

"Well, pull it out... and all the best, Phil." He was tired.

All the best!! My heart sank when the doctor said this. But in all fairness, he stayed on the phone throughout the ordeal.

I decided to stay the remaining part of the night at the clinic. Thankfully, the former nurse had left everything behind - including sheets and crockery. I've always been a great believer that when you're tired, lie down, sleep, and when you get up, you'll feel refreshed. When I woke up at daybreak, I *did* feel refreshed. I congratulated myself for being so smart and then I headed back to Marble Bar.

Then I got another phone call from my boss, the Hedland nurse. She wanted to know why I hadn't just *stayed* down there. It wasn't "just" a 240-kilometre commute to Nullagine. I was expected to stay and work there every second week. What?? I was in shock! According to my job description, I was assigned to Marble Bar. Nullagine was not even mentioned to me. Why didn't they tell me I was supposed to do this? My first thoughts were: This was a *terrible* way to treat people! I shouldn't be treated like this! I have more than enough work to do in Marble Bar. That's my home! That's where I live!

This book isn't just about me so I'll only mention this once. When I was in my mid-teens, I joined the Sisters of Mercy. Yes, I was a nun. For 20 years I laboured in an orphanage doing laundry. Imagine lonely, frightened children wetting their beds every night. There was always a lot of laundry to do. Moreover, I was cut off from the outside world; I didn't read a book or even a newspaper. I had taken the vow of Obedience and I lived an austere life. Looking back, I can see that although I left the Order to study nursing, the Order didn't fully leave me.

Nursing in Nullagine was daunting. I was really, really on my own. I wondered, what am I going to do there? Then it occurred to me: If I wasn't there, they'd have *nothing*.

Surely, I'm better than nothing! So, for the next five years, I went back and forth on alternate weeks before moving completely to Nullagine.

The following stories are not necessarily in chronological order. They are my recollections of events, which I experienced over the 15 years I lived and worked in Nullagine. I have altered the names of the people. Apologies to the heroes I encountered for not acknowledging their true identities.

Readers might be frustrated from time to time when a story has no real ending. This happens because there *was* no closure. A person was sent to hospital, to a mental institution, a prison, or they just disappeared. Once they left my care, I didn't have time to investigate further. I was on to the next duty or emergency. I lived in the moment, the here and now. Welcome aboard.

PART 2

Life in the Outback

Contact Tracing

One of my important jobs involved treatment and contact tracing for sexually transmitted diseases (STDs). When I started working in Nullagine, I found that Indigenous people had been very neglected in terms of preventative programs, especially STDs. I could see syphilitic lesions on people's faces and so I reported it to the Health Department. In my earlier nursing work in a geriatric hospital, I had seen the end result of people who went insane from untreated syphilis. They were unpredictable, often violent. The Department responded immediately and sent a doctor who came that evening to stay a week with me.

This doctor was obviously very experienced with working in remote areas. There was none of this seven-day treatment of tablets or anything. We did a massive treatment then and there in the surgery. Patients would swallow the pills in front of us before they walked out. This reduced the occurrence of syphilis greatly. And together we initiated a regular screening of bloods, which I continued to perform monthly.

Blood results helped us to estimate how *long* people had been infected. When results were positive, my initial approach was to drive directly to the person and convince them to come back to the clinic with me. They were always reluctant. They didn't want to come back to the clinic and they didn't want the treatment either! I don't think they trusted white man's medicine.

I soon figured out how to, and how not to, approach people with the news. Initially, when I drove to their home I'd say, "I got a letter from the doctor about you. I need to talk to you about it." But their response was one of suspicion:

"No doctor would write a *millie millie* [paper - in this case a letter] to me."

"You got something wrong with your blood. I've got to give you a needle," I explained.

"I'm not getting any needle!" was the consistent reply. As soon as the word needle was used, they would disappear!

Over time I learned how to gain their confidence and cooperation. We would go back to the clinic and I would offer them a cup of tea. However, once I gave them the results, the usual response was one of total denial. I would convince them to accept the needle by describing syphilis as "tiny snakes" in their blood. That really scared them and so they would readily comply with treatment.

Contact tracing was another matter, however. They would lie and deny. It took world-class interrogation skills to get information from patients and even then it wasn't always the full story. For example, I questioned one woman for an entire half-hour before I learned she had been with a whitefella, that he drove a small green car, and that he *might* be on his way to Perth. "That's fine," I assured her, "But what was his name? Surely you know his name!" I insisted. "Now stop and think. You must have called him something!"

"Yes, I did," she admitted. "I called him 'Darling.'"

Early Days

In the early days I never even *thought* about going down to the pub. I was a non-drinker. But more importantly, I always seemed to get a call around 7 o'clock at night. That was often the time some Aboriginal parent would come up with a sick child. Many vehicle accidents, fights and domestic disputes happened at night as well. To cope, I developed a routine: As soon as I finished work at 5pm, I would run home and jump into bed so that I would be rested for when I got the night calls.

One morning around 11 o'clock, I walked into the pub to get a bit of ice. There were two men sitting at the bar.

They were probably miners having a day off, or something. One said to me:

"Don't you stare at me like that!"

"I beg your pardon if I was staring at you," I replied, "I'm a bit worried. I have a sick child over here."

He snorted disdainfully and waved me off like a fly. I really do think I entered into their fantasy world. Some of these men were scared of me, or so I was told later. I was working; I wasn't there to smile and flirt (normal bar behaviour) so that might have stoked the fires. Perhaps this miner thought I wasn't interested in him. Perhaps, in his fantasy world, I thought I was too good for the likes of him and so he felt rejected. Maybe he thought I disapproved of his drinking so early in the day. Who knows?

Many of the white men did not like to come to the clinic because there were so many Aboriginals (and dogs) there. Never mind that the Government provided the clinic to serve the Indigenous people! The result was that I was an unknown factor and a topic of conversation during my early days in Nullagine.

Indigenous Names

Long before she was murdered, Helen told me the inside story about her lover, Samuel, and his brother, Donnie. Although they shared the same legitimate parentage, the lads gave the health authorities two different names. One said his surname was Moore, while the other larrikin said his name was Campbell.

The Government did not commence effective and relatively true documentation for the Indigenous desert people until the 1970s. Forget census taking! It was actually through the employment of community welfare officers and community nurses (like me), who were given the task of collecting personal and health information from patients, that the data-collection system began to evolve.

It was during the initial attempts at census taking that the two brothers gave different surnames to trick the whitefellas. They wanted to see, with all their paper and pens, how long it took the whitefellas to discover that they were brothers. No one ever did!

Nabaroo

Names are very important to Australia's Indigenous people, and they reflect the complexity of their culture. Each person has an Aboriginal name and a name that signifies their Aboriginal relationship. They also know *when* it is the correct time to use each of these cultural names.

Cultural names are difficult for non-Indigenous people to pronounce correctly. Normally during interaction with non-Aboriginals, whitefella names are used. Indigenous people give their children a wide variety of Anglo-Saxon names to try to prevent them having to be 'Nabaroo'.

This is where the complexity really kicks in. Nabaroo is a name given by the Indigenous community to an Aboriginal person who shares the same 'whitefella' name as another Aboriginal person once he has died. I'll explain: Imagine there are two Indigenous men with the same whitefella name - let's call them both 'Peter'. Imagine one of the Peters dies. When this happens, the name Peter cannot be spoken again. They don't want to stir the spirit of this dead person. To this end, the surviving Peter (as well as the deceased) is henceforth referred to as Nabaroo. Within a community, it is possible to have several people called Nabaroo.

Before I understood this, I made the mistake of asking about one of my patients. His friend put his fingers to his lips to signal that I shouldn't speak. He then came forward and whispered softly in my ear so that I would know the identity of Nabaroo. It was yet another example where I was expected to somehow know this already.

Beyond the Call of Duty

Not long after I permanently moved to Nullagine, I saw a child sitting in the gutter opening a tin of sardines with a rock. Edna was 10 years old. She was dirty and dishevelled, and her hair was matted with dust. I asked her why she wasn't at school and she answered, "I went to school this morning and the teacher told me, 'Get out. You stink. You can't stay here.'"

Edna must have been hungry because she didn't look up but kept hitting the tin can, trying to get it open. I told her I'd get a tin opener from the pub but she said, "Don't worry, it will come," and she persisted hammering with a rock.

As I stood watching her, I was horrified by her condition. Her clothes and hair were filthy. The nits in her hair were fat and numerous. They were ready to drop onto her shoulders. I decided something had to be done. This wasn't right. I began by scouting around for resources and discovered that the school's toilet block had a shower, a laundry tub and a washing machine. So, I went to the school principal and told him that a child had been turned away from school because she was told she stank. He explained that this was correct: "Under the education rules, we don't have nits or scabies."

No wonder attendance at school was poor! Back in those days, most of the Aboriginals around Nullagine drank heavily and hygiene was not a priority. They lived in humpies (lean-tos) and washed in the river. However, after six years of drought, the river was dry. Consequently, the children went to school dirty, their heads full of nits, and their legs were often covered with sores. Even when a child decided to go to school, the teachers would send them away because scabies and nits were contagious. As the principal pointed out, "Teachers have an obligation to send the child away."

"Well, I want to do something about it," I said.

"At last! That sounds wonderful," he cheered.

As the community health nurse, I reckoned that my responsibilities covered all aspects of community life, including serving as the school nurse. I thought an important part of this role was to encourage children to go to school. Yes, I went beyond the call of duty. I started by going to various Aboriginal camps and gathering up all the children's clothes that I could see lying around in the dirt. I took them back to the school and washed them.

My next step was to take my Health Department 4WD vehicle to the camps so that I could collect the children and take them to school. While the older children showered, I washed the little ones in the tub. They would then dress in the clothes that I had previously washed. I'd like to point out that their clothes were little more than rags. Although their clothes were thin and worn out, the children never noticed how shabby they were. Indeed, there were times when I could not send the small ones to school after I bathed them because they had arrived only in a singlet and I had no pants for them to wear!

When several of the students told me they were hungry, I started giving them cereal, a slice of bread and a cup of tea for breakfast. Over time I taught the children how to make lunches, how to sit at the table and how to eat their breakfast with a spoon. When they were at the table, I really encouraged good manners. I'd tell them that if a whitefella was to take them out to dinner when they got older, they would know how to act. The children excelled in good manners, learning to say 'thank you' and 'please'.

For the first two years, I paid for the food and laundry detergent out of my own pocket. The school in Nullagine accommodated forty children but because four of the students were white, it was not classified as an "Aborigine School", which meant I was not able to get any funding.

Thankfully, two dedicated teachers came to work at the school and they were very supportive of my efforts. One had trained in the SAS [Special Forces] for ten years. He decided to go to the Aboriginal reserve on pension days and ask the parents for anything they could afford in order to help pay for their children's breakfast and lunch. This was a great help because I could include fruit and better fillings for their sandwiches.

The parent-contribution program came to a stop after a visit from a Health Department doctor. "If the newspapers got ahold of this, they'd be here in a flash!" He warned us that the Aborigine Society would be critical and the teachers could get in a lot of trouble. They might even lose their jobs.

Although the food-funding initiative ended, it wasn't long before these same teachers found uniforms for the students to wear. At last! The children had decent clothes! I put each pupil's name on their uniform. It gave students such confidence and sense of well-being! Their very own set of nice clothes! At the end of each school day, the pupils returned their uniforms to me (so I could wash them) and I would give them a delicious ice block as a reward. "Don't ever ask about the funding for the uniforms," I was advised. So, till this day I don't know how the teachers made this important component possible.

I know for *certain* that my hygiene program resulted in higher school attendance with the Indigenous children. We had a big alcohol problem in the town. It was the drinking hole for other tribes who'd come in for that purpose. Despite this, we achieved 100% attendance at school. And there was never any petrol sniffing in Nullagine. Moreover, other children started coming up from Jigalong (250 km away) to our school because they had heard how well students were doing. I call that success, don't you?

At one point, the police (the only officer in town) also went beyond the call of duty. He organized basketball games after school (I helped to referee). On Sundays, he occasionally organized races for the young ones. It was endearing to watch because competition was not valued by the Aboriginal people. When the children were racing and one was left behind, another child would go back and grab the hand of the slower one so they could all cross the line together. They were all winners! Correction: *We* were all winners!

After I retired, things changed. I heard on the news that the government was unable to get Indigenous children to go to school. I wrote a letter to the Minister of Education and suggested that they get an older Aboriginal to be responsible for transporting the pupils to and from school. Children need encouragement and small children need someone to take them. (In Nullagine they only went to grade six). I suggested that the driver's reward could be a petrol voucher financed by banks that offered financial support for worthwhile community projects. Money was often converted into grog, so agencies backed off from paying for services. However, the Aboriginals were passionate about their cars. Petrol vouchers and/or new tyres were a valued source of motivation. I explained how this could help to solve the truancy problem.

I received a long-winded letter back giving reasons for why this was "not possible". The Minister of Education dismissed my suggestion. Not possible? In Nullagine we achieved a 100% school attendance record for nearly ten years! Perhaps people need to review their expectations and go beyond the call of duty.

Stumpy and the Dead Women

Around 4am I heard someone outside my bedroom window calling my name, "Philla! Philla!" Rising from my bed I looked out and saw Stumpy, an old Indigenous lady who always wore a long skirt. She spoke many languages of her own people. Stumpy never trusted whitefellas and she knew very little English.

"Two *wandi* [women] dead in creek." She pointed and added, "You betta go now!"

"Are you sure they're dead?" I asked.

"Yair, they floating in creek. On top of water."

"Come in Stumpy," I said. "Have a cup of tea."

They were dead so there was no urgency. I also knew that there would be lots of work for me. I would have to collect the bodies, complete Death Certificates, notify the police and RFDS, and contact the undertaker. Stumpy was happy about the tea and bread, but she did not speak again. Then she left and wandered off towards the store.

The creek was less than a hundred metres away. I drove the Health Department truck there and reversed it into the creek where I could see two bodies floating around. The two women's skirts had caught the wind and were ballooning out like sails. They were floating like small yachts!

Wading into the water, my intention was to grab a leg and float the dead person into the back of the truck. I had just put my two hands around a leg when an almighty shout came out of the 'dead' lady:

"Hey! That leg broken!"

"Is that you, Nettie?" I asked in surprise. "Stumpy told me that you were dead!"

"You be dead if you touch my fucken leg again!" Nettie warned me.

I then went over to the other woman and said, "Laura Lee, are you alive?"

"Yair, I'm breathing," she responded.

I managed to float them both into the back of the truck. I put a pillow under their heads and then drove them to the clinic. I soon found out what had actually happened: The women had been drinking and fighting. Nettie had taken a stick and fractured Laura Lee's arm before falling down drunk. Seeing her advantage, Laura Lee then took a brick and smashed Nettie's leg. Then they both started to cry.

Laura Lee explained: "We sisters, you know. We had big fight. Dragged ourselves to the creek. Nettie said the cold water will stop the pain. She right, you know. Then the wind came. Made our skirts blow out. With our hand, we could stir ourselves around. Nettie said, 'Hey, Laura Lee, we floating!'" By using their skirts as sails, the women were able to avoid floating into the flooded river. "Then that old Stumpy waded through the water. She said nothing to us." (Bear in mind Stumpy assumed the women were dead).

Nettie sang out from the back of the truck, "I knew Stumpy tell you, Philla! I knew you'd come!"

On examination in the clinic, I saw that Laura Lee's arm was badly broken and that Nettie had a broken leg. I applied a cast to each of their broken limbs and radioed the RFDS for advice. The doctor said, "We will see them when we fly out to Jigalong tomorrow. We will do a quick stopover on our way there. Just bring the patients to the airstrip."

The next afternoon I drove the women to the airstrip where the doctor checked them and offered to take them to the hospital in Port Hedland. They both refused. "No, we stay here with Philla," they each insisted. The nearest hospital was many miles away from their community. It would be difficult to get back, to return home afterwards. Besides, the hospital was full of whitefellas.

The Snake Pit

Just before entering the "town" of Nullagine, at the side of the road was a windmill that pumped water. Passing tourists and the local people would fill their water drums from it. Unfortunately, tourists were not aware that the water had to be boiled before drinking it and they would suffer from severe diarrhoea.

Many formal complaints were made about the well to the local Shire. After several years, the windmill was removed. I am not sure how that was done. All that I noticed was that the blades and the tall structure were gone and the well hole was covered with an old iron bed frame.

Many months after this "remedy", the senior constable ran into my clinic calling me to: "Come! Quick! I need your help with the little kids!" This was a good copper. He was always kind and fair to the Indigenous people and concerned for their welfare. Instead of lying down in the extreme heat of the day, he was doing a patrol of the town in his truck. This was a man who never panicked. Hearing the urgency in his voice, I went to fetch the emergency bag. "Leave that! Jump into my wagon. I can't do anything with the kids, they will not take any notice of me! You'll see what I mean when we get there."

We did not have to travel far to get to the old windmill – maybe 200 metres. As we drove up, I saw a cloud of dust so I assumed that the children were fighting with one another. However, once we arrived, I could see why the policeman was unnerved. There were several snakes on the ground and another flying through the air. I could see five very happy, excited Aboriginal kids aged between three and four years old. They were doing their version of a corroboree! Their little legs shifted back and forth while their feet stomped the dirt and kicked up red dust.

The children had moved the iron bed frame from the mouth of the old well. They had found a safety pin and a very thin piece of rope. They were hanging the rope down into the well and were fishing for snakes! And, yes, they were successful in catching them.

Somehow a deadly king brown had latched onto the rope. The children pulled the snake up and threw it into the air. When it landed near them, the children showed no fear; they laughed, jumped over the snake and screamed in delight as they danced their corroboree.

When we arrived at the well, there were three snakes writhing on the ground. As the little tykes were jumping on the ground at wonderful speed, the snakes were smart enough to hastily scramble into the scrub. Just as we got out of the police car there were great squeals of delight. They had caught another snake and they threw it into the air. I too jumped in the air as the snake landed near me!

The children were so happy to see me - thinking I had come to join in their play. "Philla, *chilla* [snake]!" There was such joy on their faces as they ran and jumped over the snakes.

Concerned for their safety, I said to the senior constable, "They're hysterical! They will not listen to anything." I grabbed his arm and yelled, "Grab one child at a time and lock them in the front of the police wagon. Then we can go back and grab another two."

Then suddenly up came another snake through the air. The snake was a little stunned when it hit the ground but then quickly rose to a striking position. The children certainly moved out of the way faster than I did. Fortunately, the snake missed its target - me!

Although the children were on such a high with excitement, they showed no annoyance at being locked in the police wagon. When I got the last child into the vehicle, I jumped in the front with them. They then began to speak to each other in their tribal language bragging how they were greater than the snakes. The senior constable looked down the well and said that there were maybe another ten snakes down there, all very angry and hissing.

Ordinarily, I would have taken them to the clinic and given them an ice block. However, given the seriousness of the situation, we drove straight to the reserve with the police's blue light flashing. The officer was out of the vehicle in a flash. He meant business!

"These children are not to go back to town today! There are a lot of snakes at the windmill and the kids have been playing with them!" The senior constable wanted time to fix the situation and to lodge a formal complaint with the Shire about the safety hazard.

The children, by contrast, had jumped out of the wagon and spoke excitedly in their tribal language to their parents. What an adventure for them! The parents started to laugh!

"This is no laughing matter! Those children could have died!" The senior constable was still frazzled. After all, he felt responsible for the town and the welfare of the people.

The parents became serious and hung their heads. The Aboriginals were experts at facial control, especially in front of the police. They really wanted to show their respect for this good copper and they could see that he was upset. But after we left, I know full well that they would have resumed laughing and retelling their stories around the fire that night.

Dinner Date

During the first two years of commuting, I never went socialising at the pub. I didn't drink and everyone else did. In my view, they didn't have a whole lot to talk about, and there was no television at that stage. But I think I *fascinated* them. I was definitely apart from them: I could get up and work while they'd be drunk, having fits, or having a fight and trying to kill each other.

I'm convinced they never *ever* saw anybody who didn't drink. It was said that if someone who didn't drink went up north, it was only a matter of time until they did. And people left the north because the drink had gotten hold of them. It was commonly believed that *nobody* could survive up there unless they drank. But people had seen me for years and I still was not drinking. They thought they could change me; that they could get me to drink.

Friday was Fish 'n Chip night at the pub. It was a popular social occasion, I later discovered. Jack, a fine-looking gold miner, came up to the clinic where I worked and lived and he asked to take me to dinner. I naively accepted.

I went straight from work. (It was just across the road). I entered through the back door of the hotel because it led directly into the restaurant. I didn't drink so I saw no reason to wade through the crowd in the bar.

As I sat down, the publican came straight away with a bottle of champagne. He immediately opened it, and I said, "No! No, don't do this. I don't drink alcohol."

"Yes, Yes," he insisted, "Jack said I have to look after you, if you came." Some time after, I learned that a miner had sold the champagne to the publican who then charged Jack double ($30) for it.

The publican left and in no time a server, Fiona, arrived with a lemon drink. I was thirsty and took a big gulp, but immediately spat it onto the floor! It was repulsive! Ugh!!

"I think it's poison! There's something *wrong* with this drink," I explained. I asked for a lemonade and when it arrived, I sipped it *very* cautiously. Again, it was dreadful so I said, "You've got to tell Tony [the publican] all these drinks have gone off!"

"They put three shots of vodka in it," Fiona whispered, "They said not to tell you, that you wouldn't notice." Imagine! A non-drinker wouldn't notice *three* shots of vodka!

I had been up since 4am and had a sandwich for lunch

at 11am. It was now 7:30pm and my date had not arrived. No Jack! I was really hungry by this stage and decided not to wait any longer. I asked Fiona, "Any chance of a lamb chop?" (I didn't know about Fish 'n Chip night). Anyhow, I ordered a meal with chips and vegetables.

The whole time this was going on, I could see people opening the door between the pub and the restaurant. They seemed to be peeping at me. As if I couldn't see them! I would give a little wave and they would quickly shut the door! I was wondering, do they want to come in and have dinner? I asked the publican when he arrived back at my table, but he said, "No, no. Don't you worry about them."

Although I had ordered meat, he brought me a plate of prawns. "Have this as an entrée," he said.

I didn't eat prawns in those days, so as I started to peel them, I was thinking, 'Oh, I really don't want this.' That's me all over. I'm fat because I couldn't say no to people. ("I've made this for you," so I'd eat it). Now, if you give something to me, I'll put it in the bloody bin! But back then, I was thirsty, hungry and more compliant.

Just as I was peeling the prawns, Jack staggered in. He was drunk. I knew from my training, there were six levels of drunkenness. And he was pretty drunk. Jack saw what I was doing and grabbed my plate and lifted it away from me. I think some of the prawns flew on the floor!

"Don't eat that!" he cautioned, "I owned a fishing trawler, and I don't like the look of those prawns."

"But I'm so hungry!" I was close to begging.

"Don't worry, we'll get you something else," he

promised. "You'll be sick if you eat those prawns. I *know* about prawns."

As we waited, I took the bottle of champagne and tried to pour Jack a glass. "No, no!" he protested and covered the glass with his hand. "I'm strictly a beer drinker!"

After the meal ended, I got up to go and realised that Jack was too drunk to stand. So I said, "You stay here and I'll go."

"I think that would be the wisest thing," he agreed.

• • • • •

I probably wouldn't have given this dinner date a second thought if it hadn't been for the server, Fiona. I had always been good to her. Her father used to belt up her mother and Fiona would come and stay with me. This had gone on for a couple of years by this point. She was now about 16 years old.

About three months after the dinner event, Fiona came to talk with me. "I know I should have told you. I feel so guilty," she confessed. "That night down there, there was a big bet at the bar. The miners wagered that they could get you down to the pub for a dinner and Jack would be able to give you a kiss good-night."

I think Fiona felt shamed that she hadn't warned me they wanted to get me drunk. I also think the bet involved more than just a pub meal and a good-night kiss. By getting drunk himself, I'm sure Jack was trying to protect me from more than just a few bad prawns.

Alone with a Murderer

The police came to my Nullagine clinic to ask if they could borrow the Health Department's vehicle. They said that there had been a murder in the Jigalong Aboriginal Community. They anticipated that if tribal members saw the police vehicle coming, his family would hide and assist the perpetrator. The police said, "We know who did it – it was Nabaroo." I thought for a second that using the clinic vehicle was not a good idea. However, I said yes. The police got into the clinic vehicle and left in a flurry of red dust. They had to drive nearly 250 km from Nullagine to Jigalong (each way) on rough red-dirt roads.

Just as it was getting dark and I had barely sat down to eat my simple dinner, I heard a timid knock on the door. When I opened the door, I found Nabaroo standing there! I tried to respond as though he had just popped in for a visit. "Come on in," I said gently. "I am just eating. Come share what I have. You need a cup of tea?" Putting on the kettle I was aware that he had stepped inside and had closed the door. I thought that we never know when we can upset someone unwittingly. Was I on the hit list? I hoped not.

How on earth did he get here? In those days, when things really went wrong, Aboriginal people would come to Nullagine to hide. They usually stood on the dirt road and waited for a truck to come by. Drivers *always* stopped because a person left on a bush road would die of thirst if no one stopped to help them. Hitchhikers would get onto the load at the back of the truck, and cling to the tie-downs as they made the journey to our town. I reckoned this is how Nabaroo made the long journey to my door.

"Come, my darling, come sit down. You look tired." I spoke calmly and softly. Nabaroo appeared to be in a trance. He was staring at the floor and his clothes looked as if he had lived in them for the past year. His wild, woolly hair was covered in red dust. I placed the tea on the table.

Without looking up he eventually said, "I shot one of the Crofts."

"Well, don't worry," I replied. "Do you want me to go and help him? Where is he?"

Nabaroo said, "He dead. Finished. He in Jigalong."

"Well, he must have made you very angry," I replied in the most calm and caring voice that I could muster. At this stage, I knew there were no police in Nullagine because they were 250 kilometres away planning to arrest him.

As well as being a registered nurse I was also psychiatrically trained. During my psychiatric nursing, I had worked in some very serious lock-up wards with the criminally insane. However, in the psychiatric-ward situation, I always had the most powerful backup team if we were ever in trouble or danger.

I sat there for an hour or more with Nabaroo sobbing, staring at the floor, blowing his nose, and gulping down tea. There were some extraordinary silences as we sat there together. Suddenly I heard a knock on the door. It was the police!

I went to the door and without saying anything I rolled my eyes around as if I was having a severe seizure. The police, because of their training, picked up on my eye rolls. Without verbally greeting the police, I turned my back to them and called to Nabaroo in a loud voice:

"Nabaroo, I do not know why the police are here. But it would be wise to tell them your story. You know how they like it when you come to them first and they get the real truth - the way it happened, before anyone else says silly things."

The police said, "If you have something to say to us, Nabaroo, come with us to the police station."

Nabaroo stood up and walked out to the waiting policeman. Nothing else was spoken.

Useful Snakes

A scruffy whitefella walked into the clinic saying matter-of-factly, "I have just been bitten by a snake."

"Show me where," was my first response. Then, "What time did this happen?"

"Well, I'm camped in the bush an hour's drive from here. So, 20 seconds before that."

I checked the wound site and he certainly had two decent-looking puncture marks on his leg. However, his health observations were normal; that is, his pulse, blood pressure, respirations and temperature were normal.

At that time the clinic had no satellite phone so I could not make direct contact with the RFDS in Port Hedland to discuss his case. The phone that was situated in the clinic had extremely poor reception and made a noise similar to that of a flock of magpies. I stood looking out the window while I was trying to connect with the RFDS by phone. I could see two old, very dusty Indigenous men sitting on the fence.

I asked the patient, "May I go and ask those old men outside about your snake bite? It is always important to identify the snake."

The patient nodded, with an anxious look on his face. After all, like many whitefellas he didn't respect the local Aboriginal people because alcohol abuse was prevalent in the town.

I greeted the old men with their traditional greeting, "Where you fellas from?"

"Kimberley way," they answered.

"Please come and help me," I said. "I have a man who says he has a snake bite."

Very calmly they slid off the fence saying, "Okay."

After shaking the white man's hand, they looked at his leg. "This one [the snake] about this long," said one of the Aboriginal men showing a distance of 30 centimetres with his hands. "He a green one, about this thick," he said, now showing the thickness of his thumb.

The whitefella replied, "Yes, yes, how can you tell all that?"

With that, their serious faces burst into laughter and they spoke in their own tribal language to each other. The old men were so happy one would think they had won lotto!

"Well, we know that snake," they said. "Long time ago. Long, long time. In the old days when the black people had big hair. You understand big, *big* hair?" One said, raising his hands above his head to illustrate the volume of hair. "Well, they put that little green snake into our hair and he eat up all the nits! Yair, he eat all the nits!" They laughed and clapped their hands and assured my patient, "You goin' to be all right, young fella. No worries."

They shook his hand and went outside laughing and shaking their head from side to side. They had really enjoyed making a precise and valid diagnosis. Their serious faces burst into wonderful smiles showing very strong white teeth. They spoke their language to each other for a while.

"I believe them." I said to the patient. "I would listen to them. Your blood pressure, pulse and respirations are normal. You should be showing serious signs of poisoning by now. What are your thoughts on what you want me to do - considering I cannot reach any medical doctor for advice?"

The whitefella looked at me and said, "Well, I feel calmer now, especially when those old blackfellas made us all laugh. The Kimberley mob are smart, you know. I will go over to the pub, have a few drinks and a smoke, and then go home to the camp."

The Burial of Eve's Baby

This is the worst of these stories. I still get angry when I think about it. An Indigenous woman, whom I'll call Eve, had a baby that died and had to go to the coroner. After about two months the baby was returned to Nullagine to be buried. Poor old Eve, she had a terrible life. More than once she came to the clinic because she had been held spread-eagle and pack-raped. She was a bit slow, but oh, they gave her a hard time. Eve deserves a whole chapter, really.

Anyway, her baby was due to be buried at 8am. I remember it was a Saturday because I didn't need to get the children to school. When I came down to the clinic around 6:40am, I could see about six of Eve's family members sitting in the park. They had washed and cleaned themselves like you wouldn't believe because the red dust out there was terrible. Simply terrible!

When I walked into the clinic, the grandfather came over to me and said that the baby had already been buried. "It can't be!" I replied. "Did you go without me?"

"No, when we came to sit in the park," he explained, (Bear in mind none of them had clocks), "the funeral car came back from the cemetery. It was empty. No coffin."

I just couldn't believe that this could happen so I jumped into my vehicle and went to the cemetery, which was only a kilometre away. Surely, he had it wrong! But to my horror, I saw the little grave and the fresh dirt. The baby *had* been buried!

I got in my truck and drove back to the clinic. I was so angry. God, I was angry! I went into the office and I rang the Flying Doctor. (I rang the Flying Doctor every time I was angry). And he said, "There is nothing you can do now. So, take them up and let them say their prayers. And *don't show* them how angry you are."

I followed the doctor's advice and took Eve and her relatives up to the cemetery. They spoke softly in their tribal language and the women covered the fresh grave with rocks, as was their custom. They said lovely prayers and things like, "When we go by, we'll wave. We'll sing out to you." They also said, "Now, you're not to come down and worry Mummy" and "You're not to come to town and worry us because we have to still keep living." They provided comfort by offering promises such as, "You stay up here and every time we go to Newman, we'll sing out to you."

I knew from past experiences that every time we went past the cemetery, the Aboriginals would cheer. They would put their arm up and wave. I never really made the connection that they were waving to the spirits of the dead.

"You'll be alright up here." They promised the infant. Then they named all the young people that were buried around. "And she's your relative," and "That's your sister," and "They'll look after you." Such wonderful words of comfort!

I could detect no anger or resentment although the authorities had treated them so appallingly! How could they have gone ahead and buried the baby without the family being present? By contrast, I was so angry, I could hardly speak. After this, I went to the Shire and asked him how could this have happened! "You *buried* that baby!"

The Shire man said, "Ah, yes. It was very hot and the undertaker arrived quite early so we got into town at 6 o'clock. And we said, 'Well there won't be anyone for this one. We may as well go and bury it now.'"

"Ah!" I responded, "And if *you* had a baby that died, you'd think, 'Oh, I won't bother to go to the funeral.'"

"Why are you talking to me like that for?" he asked. "Of course, we would."

I think I just swore at him and left. About a month later, a letter came to me from the coroner stating that there were only two signatures on the burial certificate and, as you know, there should be three. 'I know you are very busy, so could you please fix it up for me as I know you understand that this needs to be done,' he wrote.

I took the certificate around to the Shire and showed him the letter. There was *no way* I was signing that document!

"What are we going to do?" the Shire man asked me.

"Well, knowing you, you'd be up to forging it! That would be your standard - go burying a child without their relatives there!" I answered. Then I just walked out. It gave me great pleasure to put the responsibility back on his shoulders.

This is the very definition of oppression. The Shire man was as casual as if I had said that I had gone to the store and bought a bag of chips. He actually said, "I don't know what you're getting so excited about." Why didn't these Aboriginals get angry? Someone once suggested, "Because they get used to it."

Jimmy: An Old Goldminer

Jimmy had been a soldier in the Great War (yes, WWI). He had some dengue-fever problems and he wore a brace on his right leg. Nevertheless, he had a one-man gold mine. It was 40 kilometres out from Nullagine. Not many people knew exactly where his mine was.

When a person drove into his camp the first thing that they would see was a tin shed, with doors opening at both ends. This served as his home. Outside, there was a tin bucket suspended high in the air with a rope attached to the side of the shed. That was his shower! An "A-frame" covered with old potato sacks stood about twenty metres away. That was his pit toilet.

Inside, his tin shed had a cement floor, a very old iron bed with a mattress that drooped so much it looked like a hammock. On the bed lay his shotgun and it was loaded at all times, so he told me. There was also a table with sugar, tea, flour, Holbrook sauce, cans of baked beans, and many other groceries on it. There was a sink that drained directly onto the ground outside. The water would immediately disappear into the hot, dry soil.

"Why do you keep that gun loaded?" I asked.

"Well, if I have a king brown [poisonous snake] crawl in, it's easy to shoot at it from the bed," he explained. "Sometimes the crows come and sit on the rafters to steal my food off the table. I just fire straight out the door. That's enough to scare them off. It's very handy to be able to defend yourself when you are lying down trying to have a rest."

In an effort to make conversation, I said, "You must have met some great characters in your time." There was a *long* silence. I began to search my brain for any interesting topic of conversation to say to Jimmy.

Just as I was about to try a different topic, Jimmy gave a big sigh and slowly said, "Oh, I have met some wonderful dogs. Yes, great dogs!"

I had to suppress a laugh when he said dogs instead of people. And then I thought, how true! Dogs were central to the lives of the people in Nullagine. Me included. Ping was my favourite pet. He was a dingo and incredibly intelligent. Whenever there was a call-out at night, he would leap into the back seat and keep guard. If he heard or saw cattle or kangaroos on the road, he would give a low growl. I can't count the number of times I owed my life to that dog!

So, turning back to Jimmy, I said, "Pleased to hear that. I love dogs." Then, I added, "Tell me some stories of your early days in the Outback."

Jimmy told me this story:

"I returned from the war and came north in the early '30s looking for gold. I was on my way to town when I came across two Irish fellas. They had set up a roadblock on the old Ant Hill Road. When I drew near, they waved for me to stop. 'Come and have a drink,' they said. 'Come on you, get out of your truck and drink with us.' Sure enough, the roadblock was constructed out of cases of grog!

"Their faces were unshaven and rather grim. One shouted at me: 'We got £80,000 worth of gold from our mine. We went to Perth and loaded up our truck with this. We stop everyone and ask them to have a drink with us. Can you think of a better way of spending the gold?'"

New Policeman in Town

It was around 11pm and I was at home writing a letter to a friend when I heard a big bang on the screen door. A very tall policeman just walked straight in and said, "I am the new police here. I heard about you."

All I could think was, 'How dare you! It's late and I didn't invite you in!'

He continued, "I came to tell you that I do not love the Aborigines like you do. I have heard how generous you are. I will not be like that. And I want to get that very straight with you."

"What a lovely compliment to be told what other people say about me," I replied sarcastically.

He then turned and walked out of the house.

Several weeks later some children came to tell me that a woman from the Kimberley was crying loudly. Her husband had taken their baby and had locked himself in a room and refused to open the door. I went and spoke to the distressed mother. The baby was only six weeks old and needed to be fed. Her husband was "full drunk". I went with her to the police station and found this new senior constable standing near the waist-high wire fence that bordered the jail. I explained the situation to him.

His reply was directed to the mother, "Did he hit you?"

She answered, "No, he is drunk and silly."

The senior constable answered, "Then I can do nothing."

This reaction from the police angered the mother. "Fuck you! You don't care about us blacks!"

The copper jumped the wire fence, twisted her arm up her back and marched her into the jail. Running after him I shouted, "You can't do that! She has a baby to feed!"

"Yes, I can. Swearing at a policeman is an offence."

I went to the reserve and knocked on the door where the husband was. "Phil here! I've come to get the baby." The door opened immediately. I asked for the baby and he gave me the infant. I then told him what happened. The husband then wanted to go and fight the policeman. With great difficulty and with the help of four other men, the husband settled down. The consequences would have been dire had the drunk husband gone to settle the score with this senior constable. I took the baby to the police asking if the mother could feed the hungry infant.

His reply was, "No babies. Not allowed!" He disappeared into his house.

I went around to the side of the jail where he could not see me and I pushed the baby under a hole in the fence. This was not a simple procedure. After the baby was fed, I then had to get the baby back from the mother through the same hole in the fence.

The officer released the mother around 4pm. She came over to my house to collect her baby and told me, "He released me. I signed some papers and he released me." The mother did not want to see her husband. She asked me to help her return to her native Kimberley.

I drove her and the baby to town. There was no public transport. Fortunately for her, a truck driver was passing through and he took them to Port Hedland. In this remote area, it was common to get a lift with a truckie. In fact, I relied on them to take pathology samples to Port Hedland Hospital.

The next day, the policeman came and said there was a warrant out for her arrest.

"Where is she?" he asked me. Me!

I shrugged my shoulders and replied, "I haven't seen her today at all," (which was the truth).

No doubt, the senior constable would have called Derby and issued a warrant for her arrest. At the time, he would have learned her address in the Kimberley. However, I never heard what actually happened to her.

Samuel and the Postal Service

Despite being a drinker, Samuel was a very clean, handsome fellow who came up from Jigalong (a dry state) with his father to be nearer to other family members. I enjoyed talking with Samuel because he had the best command of English amongst the Indigenous locals.

One day I asked Samuel to post a letter in the mailbox for me as he was on his way to the store. I thought it was a simple request. Several weeks later I saw some paper blowing on the road that looked like my writing. On examination, I knew it was my letter, the one meant to go in the mailbox. Seeking Samuel out, I confronted him with the evidence.

He looked at me innocently and said, "Well, I opened it. And nothing made any sense to me. So I ripped it up and threw it away. Why? What did you want to tell me?"

"Samuel, I didn't want to tell you anything! You were supposed to post it." I said in exasperation.

"What that mean, *postit*?" he asked. Samuel had no idea how the mail system worked! He had never heard the word 'post'.

The Boys Not Taken

Robert was a whitefella, a miner who made a fortune by fossicking for gold in the Outback. When I met him, he was probably in his fifties but he had been a miner for decades. Whenever there was a heavy rain, he would hire a couple of Indigenous men to come panning for gold in the streams. The Aboriginals have incredible eyesight and they were more adept at spotting the glistening light that gold reflected in the early morning sun.

One time, as Robert recounted, they had put their blankets and swags in the back of his pickup together with litres of water, food and camp supplies. They were about to leave town when from around the corner of the pub a welfare officer jumped out of his sedan and shouted to the Indigenous men, "I'm looking for your two boys. They're going to come with me."

The Indigenous men dropped their heads to avoid eye contact and said nothing. Getting no response, the welfare officer took a spade from the back of the truck and started hitting the blankets with it. "Where are those kids?" he growled.

Robert grabbed the spade off him and said, "Stop! You can't do that. You're welcome to look everywhere on the truck. You can check inside as well, if you want."

The officer did as Robert suggested. He rummaged through the back of the truck as well as in the cabin. Finally, he agreed that the kids weren't there and that Robert and his crew could get going.

"We headed out to the Ant Hill Road and drove about 60 kilometres to a dry creek bed. The men pounded on the top of the truck and called out to stop because this was a good place to camp. So, I did and the men climbed out. I looked around and to my amazement the two wanted boys jumped out of the truck! They were about eight and 10 years old. They weren't small so I have no idea how they were able to hide. The Indigenous men weren't surprised at all. It's something only Aborigines could do and get away with! The boys went about collecting wood for fire. I'll never know how or where they were able to hide those boys."

Robert added, "I met these boys many years later, when they were in their twenties. They laughed and took pride in the fact that they were never taken."

Outback Accident

The police called me to a car accident around 5am. On arrival, I counted six people. Of the three men in the front seat, two were dead. The centre passenger's head was lying on the driver's lap which was covered in blood. Meanwhile, the driver's hand was almost severed. In the back seat, I could see three women, all Aboriginals. Sugar had exploded and coated their faces. They were alive and their tears had eventually turned the thick sugar into sticky, toffee-coloured masks.

A whitefella in a truck had run into them three hours

previously. Because he was drunk, he had stayed in his truck on the side of the road and didn't go and tell the police. Fortunately, some local Aboriginals notified the police. Unfortunately, a young inexperienced constable, who was relieving the regular police for the weekend, responded to the call. He was extremely nervous and anxious. He kept pacing, repeatedly saying that we needed to go back into town and get more help.

I asserted, "No! They've been here too long already! We'll open the door and pull the dead out."

He answered, "The doors are jammed. It's too difficult."

There was no glass in the doors so I said, "We'll pull together. Let's go!" The door came away like a wet piece of cardboard, and we both fell backwards into the bull dust. We pulled the dead men out of the car and onto the road. Then I got the women out of the car and put them in my vehicle.

As this was happening, the constable said to me, "I can hear a child crying."

"Where? I can't see one," I said.

He looked under the passenger seat and there was a three-year-old child lodged underneath the front seat! The child cried nonstop for another three hours. I took the survivors back to the clinic. I gave a large bottle of water to the ladies to help wipe the sugar off their faces. The RFDS could not come until four hours later. This is just one example of the type of trauma Outback nurses had to deal with on their own. Night accidents were very difficult given that it can be pitch black and difficult to see blackfellas.

Reporting In

I remember the first year I was up there, my boss rang me up about 6:30 in the evening and said, "Do you have something to tell me?"

"Tell you?" I was puzzled so I asked, "What sort of thing would I tell you?"

"I think you should *know* what you should tell me."

"I can't think of *what* to tell you, but if you tell me, I'll tell you."

That's how the conversation went. Abbot and Costello would be proud.

"I just turned the radio on, and I heard there was a car accident out at Nullagine and that there was a death." Her tone of voice had gone from stern to righteous.

"Ah, yes... Yes," I concurred.

"Did you attend?"

"Yes, of course I did. And I flew two out with a Flying Doctor."

"Well?"

"Well?" I echoed - leaving out the tone of indignation.

"Well, don't you think you should ring up and tell me?"

"Tell you ... there was a car accident? I had to tell the police and I had to tell the Flying Doctor. I didn't know I had to ring up and tell you." (I submitted written reports on a regular basis).

"I'm your boss!" she reminded me.

"I'm sorry, I didn't think I had to report. I never see

you. I never have any contact with you. You're not here during all the other episodes I have. I just never thought of you as part of my life!"

"We'll have to change that. I'm your boss and you have to report to me."

"When do you want a report? When they're dead or every car accident? What part do you want me to report?"

"Don't you be cheeky with me!" she warned.

"I've got to get it straight. What part do you want me to report to you? Do you just want a report when they're dead or each time I go to a car accident? Because you're going to be woken up a few times. What time of day do you want me to report to you?"

"In the morning, when I go to work at 8 o'clock. I want you to report to me."

I told another nurse who worked in another remote area about this conversation and she said, "Do you know she has no experience out where we are? And she couldn't do what you do, Phil. She couldn't even hold a candle to you. Just relax."

When I went and told the police, he said, "My boss is like that too. Just ignore them. Just say, 'Sorry. Alright, next time,' and then forget about it."

I really *didn't* see my boss. Not only this one, but the few others I had over the years. There wasn't much changeover because it was a cushy job - especially compared with remote nursing! They would come out with somebody else every three months or so. We'd meet for about an hour, and then they'd drive off into the sunset. Unlike the

Flying Doctors, they wouldn't bring me anything, except maybe water.

In the later years, up in Broome, there used to be four days of lectures with surgeons and doctors for remote-area nurses. Our bosses *never* came to them. How could they possibly understand what we go through? That's part of the reason I was so puzzled when I got this reprimand for not phoning. In reality, we didn't spend much time thinking about each other.

Unusual Flowers

Returning from holidays I bought home some plastic flowers. One of the children, who was about 11 years old, came into the house. She stopped and stared at the plastic flowers in a vase for about five minutes.

"What are these?" she asked.

I explained simply: it may be made with paper, cloth or plastic. Those are plastic. She continued to stare as I walked back into the kitchen.

Then with a loud, appreciative voice she proclaimed, "They are very good liars!"

• • • • •

Someone once sent me a box of roses on the mail plane. I put them in the clinic where I worked, to show the children. The look on their faces as they smelt the aroma of the roses was wonderful. Then they ran off, shouting in their tribal language to their elders. I have no idea what the children called out but the older people came running into the clinic.

They too stood still when they saw the big bunch of roses. Smelling them, they laughed and talked at great speed. They went out on the veranda, calling to the others under the tree to come quickly. They all came to smell the roses.

The joy those roses gave to the community was a beautiful thing to see. They laughed and talked. Going back to smell them again and again.

I believe their ability to smell is superior, beyond anything that us 'whitefellas' could ever imagine. Remember, these were Western desert people and still strongly connected to the land.

Helen's Injured Legs

Jacob was given $2,000 by the Punmu Aboriginal Community members to drive 660 kilometres south to Newman's supermarket to buy food and other goods for them. The Punmu mob were 'true desert people'. "All full bloods!" they were proud to say, "No half-castes here!"

A number of community members jumped into the truck with Jacob to go on the shopping trip. However, when they arrived in Newman, instead of shopping they went looking around the small town and nearby bush camps to see if there were any 'brothers' around. These are Indigenous people from other areas whom they would have done Lore with. Lore refers to Indigenous sacred ceremonies, initiation, and corroborees, which have united tribal people together as strong as family. Sure enough, the Wiluna mob was in town. How happy they were to see them! Alas, they were enticed into spending the food-shopping money on grog.

I heard the story of these events from Helen, who had come into the clinic to have her injured legs dressed. This is Helen's interpretation of what happened that night. Helen said that there were about sixteen of them. The night went on with drinking, singing, laughing, tribal dancing. Then more singing. Then arguing. After many hours, one person from the Wiluna mob said nasty words about the Punmu truck that Jacob was driving. That's right: his *truck*! Then "a fella" threw a stone at the Wiluna truck (which is an act of aggression, tantamount to throwing a spear). Next, Jacob jumped into his truck and ran over the Wiluna man who had insulted his truck. He then reversed the truck and accidentally ran over and squashed Helen's legs. So now it was time for another drink, and they all cried together. They began to wail and bang their heads in mourning because the man, who insulted the truck in the first instance, was truly dead!

At 8am the police came to do the usual rounds of the town and bush camps. There they found the Aboriginal group still weeping and wailing over the dead man. The police later told me that they saw cartons of beer two metres high and cartons of Jim Beam whisky that were a metre high as well as other grog. After all, $2,000 bought a lot of alcohol in the 1980s.

Helen was flown from Newman to Royal Perth Hospital to have treatment on her crushed legs. The dead man was buried after the coroner's inquest. And Jacob, who ran him over, was sent to prison. What happened to the drive-through liquor outlet staff who had sold $2,000 of alcohol to them? Nothing! What happened to the rest of the alcohol? Who knows?

Instead of returning to her home in Jigalong, Helen insisted that she be transported to Nullagine, probably because she wanted to avoid tribal punishment. When the RFDS landed, the doctor introduced me to Helen and said, "She's got a serious injury to her legs, Phil." That is how I first met Helen.

Despite several months in the Perth hospital, one of Helen's legs had a gaping wound that was approximately 20 cm long and five cm wide and seeping pus. She attended my clinic where I dressed her injured legs for several months before there was complete healing. Though herself a victim, she would not return to her tribal home, fearing punishment. Had she returned to Jigalong, she would expect to be beaten with broom handles or sticks because, after all, she had been drinking with the Punmu and the Wiluna mobs, and she was at the scene of the death. In the Aboriginal culture, Helen was as responsible as much as the perpetrators. Why? She shouldn't be drinking, she should have stopped them (somehow) before things got out of hand, she should have prevented the man from throwing the stone, she should have ensured the money was spent on food, not grog. Helens' responsibility was endless! Why? Because in their desert culture, someone always has to take the blame.

Chased

One evening after dark I was at home writing a letter. As usual, it was hot so I had the door open but the screen door was latched. I was absorbed in what I was writing and it took me a moment to notice that someone was knocking. Actually, they were pounding on the door. Then the cursing began and I realised it was a man.

Before I could get up, he kicked in the fly-wire mesh and started to verbally abuse me as he gained entry. He had been drinking but he could still pronounce s-words. So he wasn't *that* drunk.

I never saw him before in my life, but he knew who I was. "I see you in the street loving and kissing the blacks," he said in disgust. "You're not fit to be a nurse! They should run you out of town!" He made more sounds of disgust and invented more swear words.

"What's your main problem?" I asked sternly.

"You!" he shouted.

Then he raised his fist to me. I smartly moved around the table so that it was between us. I wanted to record this confrontation so I moved towards the kitchen. But then he lunged at me so I backed off. The moment he turned his back to me, I ran out the laundry door, around the house and across the road.

As I was running, I could see that the police officer's house was in darkness so I made my way to where the Aboriginal police aide lived. I banged furiously on the window. A whisper came out of the darkness,

"Phil, go away!"

I said, "No! Let me in! Let me in! That man is after me. I think he's going to belt me up!"

"He might belt you, but he will *kill* me! I'm black!"

"No, no! Quick, let me in!" I argued in a hushed tone. My house was well lit and I could see this man moving from room to room looking for me as he screamed abuse.

"You've got to let me in!" I persisted.

"No, we can't," said the aide.

"We've got babies!" his wife added. If anything happened to the Aboriginal police aide, the family would lose their house. Maybe the children would be harmed.

The man appeared to be coming out my front door. I jumped off the veranda and ran around to the back of the aide's house where their four dogs were kept.

I was always very kind to dogs so I was confident that they wouldn't attack me. In fact, they were excited to see me and happy for a bit of human company. The four of them started jumping up all over me and licking my face. I could only hope they would protect me if that man discovered where I was hiding.

Eventually, I heard his car rev up and screech down the road. I stayed put for a while, trying to calm the dogs down. I then went very quietly back to my house. I *knew* the police aide and his wife were still at the window so I said, "I'm going now." They didn't answer.

I went back to my house. I was so annoyed that he had busted my screen door. It would take a great deal of effort to repair or replace the screen. Meanwhile, I wouldn't be able to keep the mosquitoes out. I shut and locked all the wooden doors and went to bed. Yes, nothing got in the way of my ability to sleep from exhaustion.

The next day I was down in the clinic when the man who ran the Mines Department walked in. He was a very old man who had lived there all his life. His family would have been born and bred there.

"I believe you had some trouble last night," he said.

"What trouble would that have been?" I was testing the waters.

"I believe one of our fellows had too much to drink and I've come in to say I'm sorry."

"It wasn't quite as calmly as that. He really did abuse and threaten me," I clarified.

"That man was drunk. He was drunk and people do silly things when they're drunk. And I told him I'm coming over to settle it all down. You understand drunk people. And you're very good at understanding people out here in the Outback - what it's like in the heat. So, we're square now," he proclaimed. And he walked out!

His words sounded rehearsed. When I thought more about this, I could see that the Aboriginal police aide must have reported some version of events to the police who in turn tried to "settle the matter". This third-party 'sorry' meant nothing to me. And it didn't fix my screen door!

Lore

Every year before the wet (possibly November), Lore was practised. Lore provides the rules for how Indigenous people should interact with the land, kinship and community. One aspect of Lore refers to when boys are initiated into manhood. When I was in Nullagine, the Elders would come to town and notify the police that they intended to take some boys to Jigalong to perform their traditional rites. Hundreds of men participated; tribes came down from Broome, the Northern Territory, all over. Big truck loads with the *Mabin Man* coming through. It was very sacred. Anyone who lived around the area was not allowed to go on the road unless they had special permission.

Rite of Passage
Many boys did not go willingly; they would run and hide. (Hence, the need to liaise with the police so they were not charged with kidnapping). Mothers would not intervene one way or the other while fathers accepted the ritual as a rite of passage.

The men would relay, walking the young boys until they could walk no more. The adults would walk maybe five kilometres (I don't know what distance, actually), then pass the boys to another crew to walk the next five kilometres, and so on. By the end, the last lot of men would have to drag and carry the boys. Once the lads were totally spent, that's when they did Lore.

It took years before I found out *why* they would walk the young boys so far. Exhaustion served as an anaesthetic. Lore involved physical pain. There would be cuttings to their penis, chest and upper arms. The men quite liked their scarring. When they had fights and were mutilated, they never wanted to be stitched up. They wanted to still have that scarring.

Afterwards, the boys would come back with infections, like hepatitis. A rock was used to cut their penis lengthwise. To prevent infections, the doctors talked with the Elders and gave them sterile blades; however, sometimes the cut was too deep. I had boys come into the clinic and say, "Promise, promise you won't tell anyone." And they would show me their penis. I knew these boys since they were little fellows so they had complete trust in me. Their penis would be cut lengthwise right down the middle, like a butterflied sausage. They wanted something to ease the pain. I recently met a surgeon who offers corrective surgery, which means this practice still takes place.

Tribal Justice
These annual trips were also a time when tribal justice was carried out. Payback time. Wrongdoers would be punished

according to Lore. It was remarkable how the Martu knew when the huge tray-top truck was going to pass through carrying the *Kadaitcha Man* (featherfoot, executioner) and Elders with their swags and drums of water. Every year, and sometimes twice a year, women would run into the clinic and crouch down on the floor.

"They're coming! Don't look out the window!" They told me. They believed that if any of those men looked at me, I'd be cursed.

I complied with their advice and went into my office, which had no windows. However, over the years I did peek out the window a few times when no one was looking my way. The men were scanning the pub and the store as they passed through town.

Nullagine was a small community so the truck didn't always stop, but occasionally they would stop for petrol and the women hiding in the clinic would get very scared. Was someone going to be punished?

Tribal laws were strict and punishment maintained the rules. For example, their laws concerned who slept with whom - partners could not be relatives or perhaps members of a specific tribe. Serious punishment was performed by spearing. The spear was to go into the wrongdoer's thigh. The mob would come together to form a tight circle. The one who had broken Lore would stand in the centre, arms down at his side. Never in a defensive manner. The Martu were very serious about taking their punishment. The victim would not run. The person or persons who had been wronged threw the spears. I only know the ritual was far more complicated than this, but that is all I was able to learn about it. There were serious punishments (even death) for disclosing certain secrets.

Another set of punishments often applied to women. It involved beating the wrongdoer with thick sticks and even broomsticks. Again, the mob would form a tight circle and thrash her. In the movie, *Samson and Delilah* (2009), the latter was punished because her grandmother had died. This scene clearly illustrated the huge gap in cultural worldviews. Although Delilah had taken good care of her grandmother and although the old woman had died from natural causes, Delilah was punished. Someone was to blame. I saw this with accident survivors and prison inmates. Someone must be held responsible, even if they are blameless. This is part of Tribal Justice.

Trina's Rape

I answered a knock on my front door at 2am and there stood Trina. She was naked, blood running down between her legs and dry grass through her hair. She shouted, "They pack-raped me! They held me down! All of them laughing. I want the police! Come, take me to the police!" She was hysterical. No way could I calm her.

I threw a sheet around her naked body and walked her about 50 metres to the police residence. I rang the bell. When the police officer opened the door Trina started to scream at him, telling him that she had been pack-raped. She wanted justice! She wanted him to go and get them right now! The rapists were still in the dry river bed drinking. The officer did not utter a word. Instead, he grabbed a set of keys and started to walk towards the jail. Trina quickly realised that he intended to put *her* in the lock-up. Trina yelled, "I'm the one who was raped! I don't go to jail for that!"

"What are you doing with her?" I asked. I was in panic mode!

The police remained silent. He opened the cell door, pushed Trina into the cell and turned the key in the gate. This was the worst injustice I have ever seen! This isn't how you treat rape victims! I started to speak up in Trina's defence: "You can't do this! This is terrible! Give her back to me!" I said that I would take Trina home and look after her.

The officer replied that it was *his* responsibility to keep her safe and stated that she would be safe in the lock-up as there is no guarantee that she would be safe in my house.

Trina began to cry and begged him, "Don't do this to me!"

The policeman turned and went back into his house. I felt totally helpless not being able to help Trina in her current situation. I stayed outside her cell and talked to her for a while to try to calm her. I called out to the other prisoners to ask if they could give her some clothes to cover her naked body. I knew that a lot more should have been done for this rape victim.

Cars in the Outback

It was nearly a 200-kilometre journey from the mining town of Newman to Nullagine. The road was unsealed, rough, corrugated and dusty. I was about halfway home to Nullagine when I thought I could see a plane on the road ahead of me. Thinking that some emergency had occurred, I was not too surprised to see a plane on the road. I thought that it must be the RFDS. Landing on unsealed Outback roads to attend to a motor vehicle accident did happen from time to time.

I was very surprised when I drew nearer and realised that it was an Aboriginal's car with a long plank of wood sticking out through the side windows in the back of the vehicle! That's what gave the appearance of the wings on a plane. They were travelling about 60 kilometres an hour. When I drew even closer, I could see there were two men sitting on each end of the plank that jutted out of the rear windows. They were positioned outside on the wings! The children were sitting on the floor of the car under the plank in the back seat.

When they saw it was my Health Department personnel carrier, they pulled over to the side and we both stopped our vehicles. Walking up to them I counted eleven people in the car. "Anyone like to come with me?" I asked.

Cheers went up and people greeted me with, "Philla, you got any water?" They were coated in so much dust that their skin and hair looked red instead of black! I handed the water bottle to the two men still sitting on the left side of the plank because they looked the driest. Once they had a gulp they called out to the men on the other side of the plank, "We give you a drink next!"

The driver got out of the car stretching as he spoke, "Too many people wanted to come this way so we used the wood. You want to take some kids with you?" he asked me.

The plank of wood remained in the car while the children and several women crawled out through the front seat. "Why you keeping that wood?" I asked since it was more practical to remove it.

"Oh, good for fire. It come in handy tonight," the driver explained.

I shared some more water all round. The Martu went singing their way back into 'country' just as their Indigenous ancestors had done for thousands of years. No maps, only song. Incredible!

• • • • •

Some people may have seen a programme on television about bush mechanics and how it is done by the Indigenous people in the Outback. Nothing was exaggerated in that series. When working and travelling in the Outback of Western Australia I had the opportunity to look into many Indigenous people's cars. I have observed such things as:

- There was no floor in the front of the car. The driver and front passenger just rested their feet on the side frame of the car.

- There was no backrest on the driver's seat. It was like sitting on a stool!
- The passengers in the back seat put a jerrycan behind the driver's back. Then the two children in the back seat held it there with their feet. They were about 11 years old.
- The person on the front passenger side had his arm out of the window. He was holding a two-litre cordial bottle full of petrol. Yes, it was outside the car, sort of resting on the hood. The cordial bottle had a thin plastic hose going to somewhere into the engine. Why? Because there was a hole in the petrol tank.
- Using a woman's brassiere for a fan belt was a common practice.
- Frequently the cars had no upholstery - just the basic wire coils sticking up out of the seats.
- Flat tyre? No worries! I've seen Aboriginals pack spinifex into the tyre in lieu of air!

The Satellite Dish

Up till 1989, Nullagine had no access to television. A satellite dish was needed due to the remoteness of our town. The school teachers were strong advocates for having TV for teaching and learning purposes. The town's people also thought it a good idea. They believed they would spend less time in the pub if there were televisions to go home to.

Many of us wrote letters to the Shire and to politicians. No replies and nothing happened. However, we continued to send letters consistently - especially the teachers.

Now a little diversion here. But you will see the TV is connected to this story. (Pun intended). One Friday night in the pub, where the town folk always came together to have a meal of fish and chips, someone had the bright idea to play cricket. He shouted out, "Everyone listen! Let's play cricket next Saturday! The blacks against the whites. Do you agree?"

There was a great roar from the mob, agreeing. "We will be in that!" called out folks from the black bar.

The pub was segregated. Yes, one side for the whites and the other for the blacks! The bar's benchtop separated the two areas, which explains how people could see and call to one another.

"We will let you have extra men on your side!" offered the whitefellas to the Aboriginals. The miners expected to outnumber the local Indigenous.

The Aboriginal men started to practice down at the reserve. When the following Saturday arrived, 20 whitefellas were there and so were about 45 Aboriginals. The idea of big teams was to relieve their players, because of the heat.

Many of the Indigenous were waiting to bat. One went to the Umpire and said, "You gotta stop that boy hittin, he needs to let the others have a go! Other fellas wanta turn on the bat!" The Aboriginals were not familiar with the rules of the game, but the Umpire changed the batsman and there were many smiles from all.

One of the Aboriginals fielding yelled out, "Hey! There is a plane comin. Not the Flying Doctor. But I bet it is whitefellas!"

No one else heard a plane. Someone else said, "Well it is not for us. We're here to play cricket!"

About 10 minutes later, five people, driven by the publican, arrived at the cricket ground. The game continued, with mutterings from the Indigenous. "I told you there are city people on that plane."

The Umpire went over to the group. "Who are you?" "We have just flown in from Perth. I hold the portfolio for the Arts. You requested a TV satellite. The publican told us all the town's people were at the cricket grounds. Is that right? You have the whole town here?"

"Yes! That is true," he said.

With that, the entourage burst out laughing. "You will never be supported with this number." There were only 80 of us.

The Umpire shouted out to everyone, "Hey! These are the people from the government to see if we deserve television."

The players all stopped and walked over to them. The police, the school teachers, the Shire men, the nurse (yours truly) and, most importantly, those who outnumbered the whitefellas - the Indigenous residents!

"We only support towns with 100 people. You will

never qualify." Again, the politician laughed. A few people argued. The government people put up their hand saying, "We have to go. We are on a tight schedule."

Then someone shouted (I am not sure who): "The price of the plane and travelling here could have paid for our satellite dish!" Everyone gave a mighty cheer in agreement, and we all started clapping. The politicians laughed as though they'd heard a funny joke and they departed.

Two months later, we got the satellite dish.

Encounters with Paedophilia

A three-year-old girl was standing outside the corner of the pub. She was bleeding between her legs so they took her to Hedland Hospital and the doctors said that she had stuck sticks up herself. She needed repairs to her genitals. We knew she had been sexually abused, but it took me a *long* time to find out who it was. Everyone was amazed that I didn't know. They *always* assumed that I knew. Many times and in various situations, I'd have Aboriginals say to me, "You should know. You been here a long time. You should know!" I guess they were better at using their eyes and ears than I was.

I found out that one of the local young men wanted to go out with the little girl's mother, but the mother didn't want to go out with him. So, he took the three-year old and raped her. He was never punished for that at all. There was no follow-up.

There were dreadful atrocities like that. Another woman was going with a white man. He had taken her and her 11-year-old daughter to Marble Bar for a while. The young girl, Gail, later told me that he had made advances and touched her inappropriately. They left him and came to Nullagine. I became quite friendly with the mother, but she was drunk 24/7.

One morning as I was collecting the children to bring them to school, I noticed that Gail was missing. The younger children told me the old Bulgarian with silver rings on his fingers had taken her to Marble Bar, which was around 120 kilometres away. The Bulgarian said if she went with him, he would buy her a bicycle.

I went directly to the police and asked them to do something about the situation. "He has no right to be with this child!"

They asked if I had spoken to the mother. I hadn't. "This is hearsay from little kids," the police replied and shook their heads saying, "We cannot do anything." It was a good point so I went to the reserve and woke up the mother who was drunk.

"Did you know your daughter was up in Marble Bar with the Bulgarian?" I asked.

"No, I thought she was staying with family," she said and denied any knowledge of what the children had told me.

I said I wanted to go to Marble Bar and get the child.

The mother waved her hand and replied, "You can do what you like." She was indifferent.

I returned to the police a second time and informed them that I was going to retrieve the child. The officer stood up and warned me: "You better be careful. You could be charged with kidnapping! You're not family." Indeed, it could be a serious offence since I was not a relative of the child.

I then went directly to my clinic and rang the Child Welfare Services for Aborigines, as it was known then. They said, yes, yes, they'd look into it. I rang Marble Bar again the next day and the man who was part-Aboriginal answered said, yes, he had seen the child up there. To my dismay, he then admonished *me*!

"What scandalous accusations you are making about this man! Do you realise what can happen if what you are saying is wrong?" He went on to say that I was saying some very serious stuff, and that I might face charges if I took that little girl back to Nullagine. Incredible! He reiterated what the police had said: I'm not family. Who was I to do this? I answered, I do not care. I am going to Marble Bar to see what is happening.

He then replied in a commanding tone, "Your name will end up in the newspaper. You are interfering in a family's life! You have nothing to do with this!"

I replied, "If I'm wrong, I'll be very happy to make a public apology - in the *newspaper*! But you should go there and bring the child back!"

He continued in that line of conversation about how I

was on dangerous ground. "You've got to have facts. You can't accuse people of this type of paedophilia," *etc*.

"Well, will *you* go?" I persisted. It was his job after all!

"I will look into it next week," he conceded.

Next week? That was ridiculous. Far too long. Far too long! That night the girl still didn't come home so the next morning I closed the clinic, jumped into the truck and drove the 120 kilometres to Marble Bar. It was surprisingly easy to find out where they were. I pulled up in front of the Bulgarian's house. With the motor still running, I asked myself, how will I do this? I took a deep breath and walked straight into his house. I looked at the Bulgarian and said that I'd come to take the girl home. Then I turned to her and said, "Come, Gail, I've come to take you home."

Gail ran out of the house at the speed of light. We got in the truck and the Bulgarian didn't say anything. So off we went. Gail kept repeating to me, "I knew you would come and get me. I knew you would come!" She was breathless with relief and happiness. I did not question her or complain of the trouble I had experienced when I tried to rescue her legally. Instead, we spoke of school and casual stuff.

When we returned to Nullagine, I asked her where she wanted to go. She said school so I dropped her there and went to see her mother. "I've got her. She came back with me and she wanted to go to school. Is that all right with you?"

"Oh, yes, that's good," her mother replied. "Make her go to school."

Next, I rang the Welfare (white services) in Port Hedland, and asked to speak to someone experienced with child abuse cases. To my relief, they responded kindly and showed concern. The next day they sent a professional social worker to speak to Gail about her experience. They used an anatomically correct doll and all that business, the way they do. Yes, he had certainly had a lot of sexual misconduct with that child.

Before going to Marble Bar, the police had warned me to be careful, that I could end up in court. So, when I got back, I told the police what I had done and said to them:

"I don't care what you say. If you want to document it down, I walked in the house and I took the child."

"You're braver than we are, Phil," they replied.

I don't know all the details about what happened after this point. I don't think this story was ever documented, except in police notes, perhaps. I know Welfare Services spoke with the mother and acknowledged my referral.

Evan and Outback Politics

I was looking out the clinic window, just on dusk. The sky was a crimson colour with about sixty grey galahs and twenty crows free-falling in the air thermals. Then upward they flew and again commenced their rapid descent. It was spectacular to watch. I called out to an Indigenous woman, "What are those birds doing?"

"Oh! They just playing," she answered.

Suddenly a red dust-covered sedan drove into town and stopped at the corner where Evan, an Indigenous man who worked as a labourer for the Shire, was waiting. He was one of the few inhabitants who had not lost his driver's license and so he was employed to drive around the town to collect rubbish. The white man got out of the car and handed Evan a large box and some money. For more than a minute there was a one-way conversation while the man talked and Evan stood and looked at him. Evan could speak basic English but he could not read or write. The white man got into his car and headed north. Evan stood and watched the car head out of town. He then ripped open the box, stared at the contents, then he put the box in the garbage bin and walked into the pub.

I went over to the bin to see what was in the box. It was full of brand-new glossy brochures on how to vote Liberal in the upcoming election. While I was looking at the brochures Evan came out from the pub with a carton of beer on his shoulder. He saw me pulling the papers out of the box and said, "Hey. You want those fucken *millie millie* [papers]? It's alright with me. You take them all!"

"What did that man say you had to do with them?" I asked.

"'Not too fucken sure," said Evan. "He just said, stand at the school tomorrow and give them away. And he handed me money to buy a carton of beer. Tomorrow, it's fucken Saturday! No fucken school!"

I explained that Saturday was the day we had to vote

for the government. With a great big smile, Evan replied, "'I don't know anything about those fucking things. But a real easy job for a fucken carton of beer!" And off he went with a skip in his step and the carton of beer raised high on his shoulder.

The Canadian Miner in Trouble

One thing I discovered about Nullagine: there were no bland characters! Jack, for example, was a thirty-something whitefella who was very nice, very placid. He always walked around with his shirt completely unbuttoned. At the age of 12, he saw his father hack his mother to pieces in their kitchen. When I met him, he was living in the hotel and always drinking. I'm not sure what he lived on, but everyone accepted him and gave him little jobs from time to time.

Jack used to do regular rounds and visit the one-man mining camps for a chat (and a drink). Because he went so often, I'm quite sure the old blokes would also slip him a hundred dollars in return for some help with odd jobs.

One day, Jack went to visit a Canadian who also had an interesting background. The Canuck was about Jack's age. He was big and quite good looking. He had been married and had owned a profitable service station up north. One day he came home and found his whole house had been cleared out. All the furniture, the knives and forks, everything gone! He decided he would sell the servo and go look for gold. Everyone who stopped to refuel was always going out looking for gold. The Canuck decided he needed a change, and he got it.

When Jack arrived at his camp, it was obvious the Canadian was in trouble. He was very, very sick. And he had been sick a long time. By this point, the miner had not been able to stand up for many days. Fortunately, his bed was right next to a kerosene fridge so he was able to survive by eating dozens and dozens of raw eggs.

Nullagine had the nearest grocery store but fresh produce only arrived once a week. Fresh fruit and vegetables sold out within hours so people (me included) would travel nearly 200 kilometres to Newman and do a big shop that could last for several months. This is why the Canadian had so many eggs available.

When Jack arrived at the shack, the Canuck's bed was covered in eggshells as well as urine and faeces. Jack got such a shock he came straight back to Nullagine to get me.

"Go across and see who you can get out of the pub to help us," I said to Jack.

Men just worked and worked on their mines all the time so they loved this stuff. There was no trouble finding volunteers. Two miners, one also called Jack, answered the call. He came across and pointed out, "You want to think about the dog." The Canuck had a vicious dog that would guard him and his gold. "So, you got to get the vet."

"We'll pick him up on the way," I agreed.

"No, he's in the pub. We'll get him out now."

The men explained the situation to the vet. He reckoned that if the Canuck was that sick, he wouldn't have fed his dog. Since the dog would be starving the vet decided to put sedation into some meat and use it to lure the dog away from the cabin.

The five of us piled into my Health Department 4WD and headed out to the Canuck's camp. It was late in the afternoon and all we could think about was the light. We needed to find his camp before dark. Miners usually keep a small kerosene lantern burning so that they can find their way in the dark.

"The Canuck is too sick to have a light up," Jack said, "We've got to get out there before it's too dark or we won't find him."

It was a hard place to find. No roads. No tracks. We just travelled over the spinifex. Finally, we could see the outline of his tin shed. When we arrived, the vet grabbed the meat and went over to the Canuck's truck. He tossed the meat into the back seat and the dog immediately jumped in after it. The poor thing really was starving.

Everything was going to plan. But then the vet jumped into the Canadian's truck and said, "I'm off!"

"Where are you going?" the other men yelled out.

"I'm off. I've done my job. I'm a vet!"

"Stop!" Jack, the miner, shouted.

"You're worried about the fucking light, aren't you? Well, I've still got to find my way back." It was still twilight and off he went!

With the dog out of the way, I was able to enter the

cabin. The patient was barely conscious. All I could think was, 'We've got to get out of here! We've got to get away from this place!' I had brought water so I lifted his head and gave him a drink. The Canuck grabbed my collar and pulled me close so he could whisper,

"There is a bag in there. I want you to look after it. Don't tell anyone you've got it. You look after it. Put it in a safe place till you hear from me." Then he cautioned, "There are *snakes* in there, Phil."

I went into this narrow little pantry and I saw a snake as well as the bag. It was so heavy I couldn't pick it up; I had to walk backwards and drag it out. Of course, there was no way to be secretive about it. The Canuck was delusional and near death. He had his eyes shut most of the time.

First, we had to work out how to get the Canadian into my truck. We had to use the putrid mattress as a stretcher. But as we lifted it by the corners, it collapsed and sagged in the middle like a funnel. Everything was seeping through – the slimy eggshells, the urine, the faeces. It was all messy under there. We really needed one more person. Jack, the miner, took the centre of the mattress and the other men held the ends. Boy, those men were strong!

Once they got the patient into the truck, I went over to Jack (the miner) and quietly said, "He's worried about the bag, and I can't lift it."

"You know it's gold, don't you?" he whispered back.

"I don't know what's in it," I replied, "I thought it was biscuits."

As you can see, I wasn't a very good liar. But I really

didn't think about it. I just thought it was money. As it turned out, the bag held gold bars and it took two men to pick it up.

"It's all a big secret," I said.

"Yes, and you keep it a secret too," he advised.

The men got really serious then. They were all whispering although the Canuck was unconscious in the back of the truck.

They put the gold in the front of the vehicle and when we got back to Nullagine, miner Jack came with me to my home and put the bag under the bed. "I think I'd change that position," he said.

"I will, Jack. I will," I promised. But I never moved it again. In fact, I never thought of it again.

Months later, the Canadian returned to Nullagine to collect his gold and his dog. Then he cleared out and we never saw him again.

How The Desert People Lived

It is very different from the Eastern states to the Western states. The eastern Aboriginals are far more educated, far more civilized. They have forgotten a lot of the old ways. I think if they knew the earlier culture, the ways of the desert people, most would be surprised.

Time and Money

You are probably familiar with the expression, "Time is money"; both are important, both are valued, right? The Indigenous people I first met seemed to find both concepts virtually meaningless. The local Aboriginals didn't wear watches or look at clocks. They measured time by events, like the "big blow" as when a large dust storm went through the area. "Long time, long, long time" could refer to a *thousand* years ago. I had to be flexible about setting appointments!

Money also held little value. When I first commuted to Nullagine, they lived in humpies and cooked on open fires. No electricity, no refrigeration. Desert people would hunt and eat kangaroos and goannas. On pension day, I saw adults give a four-year-old $50 to get a feed from the hotel. For many Aboriginals, most of their money went on grog. The general store was used like a pantry - until their credit ran out. One time a woman used a gold nugget she had found to buy milk from the store. I don't think she received (or expected) any change. The same thing happened with a man who exchanged a gold nugget for a slab of beer.

How They Cook

One early morning I walked down the dry river bed to find an Aboriginal man to give him some medicine. Sitting around a fire he had a *bungarra* (very large lizard) on the open fire.

"How long to cook that one?" I asked.

"All depends on how hungry you are," he replied with a belly laugh and clapping his hands.

Over the years I have noticed that Indigenous cuisine consisted of boiled or burnt, with dirt and without. If food dropped on the ground, there was never a fuss. Unlike a white man's BBQ, I would see no recriminations, no blaming, no shouting. They would simply pick the food off the ground and wipe it on their trousers or brush it with their hands before eating.

The Stars Above

If you go to the Pilbara, the *real* Outback, you will be captivated by the stars, millions of stars! Their beauty cannot be accurately described; it has to be seen! I have seen showers of stars fall like a cascade of giant diamonds. What could be more beautiful, more breathtaking?

The Martu, the true desert people, helped me to see the stars with new eyes. They don't look for the Southern Cross or Orion's Belt (see how indoctrinated we are!). The Indigenous see different things in the Australian sky, like the Emu and the Kangaroo.

Sex Education

While Lore provided a rite of passage for Indigenous males, there did not seem to be comparable rituals for females. However, it was usual to give a seven- or eight-year-old girl to old, old men. They would come into the clinic and introduce him as their 'husband'. They would run messages for him, but mainly it involved getting the billycan of water and firewood. In return, he would teach them the ways of sex. These Aboriginal people believed that in terms of sex education, it was better that an old man teach girls 'how things are done'. I can honestly say those girls knew everything possible about sex; it was part of life - like eating, drinking and breathing.

Walkabouts

Trina walked into the clinic one day and just sat down and started to talk to me:

"They say we go walkabout. Walking about all the time. That's not true! We not walking everywhere. If we come and there's water and there's food and kangaroos, we sit and we stay there. We might stay there two *years*. We don't have to go. They telling lies!"

I don't know where Trina heard this, or why she came in so distressed about it. Maybe it was about the time we got television, which was around 1990. She might have watched something on the ABC - that was the only station we had. But she was indignant:

"We stay where there's water. We stay where there's food. Then when there's too much rubbish there, we just move along and let the crows clean up the mess. That's how we live. Do they think we're mad? Why would we go?"

Keeping Cool

Living conditions changed somewhat for the Indigenous people when the Government came and built small cement houses for them. The buildings consisted of one bedroom, a breezeway and a kitchen. The Martu continued to sleep outside, but they would store their mattresses inside during the day. They also continued to cook outdoors over an open fire.

The local Aboriginals did appreciate and use the overhead fans that were installed in each house. I often saw a skinned kangaroo draped over the ceiling fan. When the fan was turned on low, the kangaroo meat would spin around. It was a great way to keep flies off the carcass! There was one drawback, however, it would splatter kangaroo blood on the walls and on the people sitting nearby. On very hot, windy, dusty days, the men would bring a water sprinkler into the middle of the room and set it on low. They would sit around talking and having a drink. "This is our water cooler." They were very happy they discovered these methods of fly control and cooling system for themselves.

Long Time No See
After 10 years of service, I started having six weeks off. It was a big break. And when I returned the people who really loved me (mainly the women) would put their arms around me and cry. Even some of the men would sob long and hard. It was an Aboriginal thing.

By custom, if relatives hadn't seen one another for months or a year, the more noise they would make and the longer they would make crying sounds. They would say, "I have been crying for you," where whitefellas might say,

"I've been thinking about you," or "I've thought about you so much." That's what the crying represented.

To a whitefella, I suppose it would seem like an artificial cry. I didn't think it was artificial. I used to cry too; I used to make the sounds. I cried because I was sad that I had been away from them. They really liked that interaction. I was part of them, without any hesitation. They were my friends, my family. I was there on my own for 15 years. My relatives were over in the Eastern states. They all had lots of children and they certainly weren't thinking about me.

Help Yourself

A Protestant Minister once told me about one of his happiest moments of being with Aboriginals in the Outback. For 15 years he drove them around to wherever they wanted to go. He took them to every funeral, to the shops, you name it. One day they asked him to stop at the store because they hadn't had any dinner. One of the women went into the shop and brought back some food. She climbed into the back seat and then she leaned forward and said,

"Here, Pastor, I bought you a sandwich."

The minister said he burst into tears and he couldn't stop crying. It was the first time any of them had ever offered him anything. He was deeply touched, overwhelmed.

"I've seen them eat chips. I've seen them eat fish and they never once offered any," he explained. It was a breakthrough moment for him. He was so emotional when he told me about this!

I heard this story when I first went to the Pilbara, so I took it at face value. After a while, however, as I became more familiar with Indigenous culture, I realised it was *his* place to just reach out and take any food that was going round. He had been around long enough to know that.

The Indigenous are straightforward people. They would have assumed that the Minister wasn't hungry. In their view, a person who was hungry would have to be super stupid just to sit there and watch while everyone else ate. What a madman! Closeness requires no formality.

One time the police told me that Aboriginals would go into my home when I wasn't there. I never connected the dots. I would be missing items (sunglasses, perfume, whatever) but I put it down to my being forgetful. A friend would complain that the beer he had stored in my fridge was missing. He had purchased a carton and there was only one left.

"You drink," I admonished him. "You forget!"

It was only later - at the Christian revival - that I made the connection.

Jason and Cathy

Cathy was educated up to the age of 14 years and spoke English well. She was confident, highly respected in her own community, and had a lovely, pleasant personality. She picked up with Jason, who was not part of her tribe. It was easy to see the attraction. He was well built, stood

180cm tall, and was a full-blooded Indigenous man. He was wonderful with little kids. I remember seeing him coming out of the pub and seeing a small child crying. He picked her up, talked with her, and wiped her tears. Very sweet. Unfortunately, Jason was addicted to alcohol in a serious way and when he was drunk, he could get angry.

Jason came to my house late one night and said, "I've just killed Cathy."

"That's terrible," I responded as sympathetically as I could muster. "I'll go down and have a look. See if she's really dead."

I asked Jason to go back home and to turn on some lights so I could find him. I explained that I would fix up my medical bag and meet him there. There was *no way* I was going to get into the truck with Jason as a passenger! He was still drunk and unpredictable.

When I arrived at the reserve, I noticed that his door was open and the light was on, as I had requested. The couple lived in a primitive one-bedroom house. When I entered the bedroom, Jason was there. He was crying and wiping his eyes with his hands. Even in the dim light, I could see blood splattered on the walls.

Cathy was lying on a thin mattress on the floor. A very dirty, heavy quilt covered her. As I moved towards her bed, I asked, "What did you hit her with, Jason?" I tried to calm the situation by speaking softly and gently. To be honest, I was also thinking of my own protection. I didn't want to be hit by the same weapon! Was it a baseball bat? If so, I intended to walk over and pick it up.

"A kangaroo jack," he answered.

Kangaroo jacks are used to raise trucks and 4WDs. This was a heavy weapon! It was made of steel and it would take a great deal of rage and strength to bludgeon anyone with it.

I knelt down to where Cathy was lying and I pulled off the doona that was covering her. There was so much blood that I initially thought that she was wearing a red dress. She had a dreadful head wound. Her eyes were closed. No movement. She was still breathing so I felt for a femoral pulse.

"Jason, she is still alive. You haven't killed her. Go get some men! We will pick up the mattress with her on it and take her to the clinic. Go quickly!"

Within minutes, we were transporting Cathy into the clinic. As I drove, Jason sat in the back nursing Cathy's head in his lap. When we arrived at the clinic, I ran ahead to open the door. With the help of three Aboriginal men, whom Jason had recruited, they lifted Cathy off the bloody mattress onto the emergency bed with gentleness, perfect timing, and powerful strength.

I followed the usual procedures for emergencies: I took her pulse, blood pressure, and respirations and tried to estimate blood loss. Time was of the essence so then I rang the RFDS and reported severe head trauma and loss of blood. I said I hadn't yet examined the rest of her. They advised me to start stitching any wounds I could see.

We were extraordinarily lucky. The Flying Doctors were only 40 minutes away because they were already picking up another patient from a station. Usually, we could expect a 2½ hour wait for their plane to come from Port Hedland. After our call, I immediately phoned the police. (It hadn't occurred to me to contact them earlier). I asked them to place lights out on the runway, which was nothing more than a grassy field, so that the RFDS could tell where it was safe to land. While we waited for their plane to arrive, Jason helped by washing the blood off Cathy's body as I kept stitching. We drove to the airstrip and Cathy was taken to hospital.

I didn't see Jason again for a long time after this incident. The police would have conducted an investigation. *Maybe* Jason served time in prison. That would explain his absence. As for Cathy, the RFDS would have returned her to her home. Later I was relieved to hear that Cathy had made a full recovery.

Daphanie and Classroom Discipline

One hot day when the thermometer registered 44°C Daphanie, aged nine, came into the clinic. She was a half-caste and her beautiful face was very red from the heat. It was a long walk from the school to visit me. She had a guilty look on her face. I ignored that and offered her a strawberry ice block.

I sat doing paperwork, but after several minutes I asked her, "Do you feel sick?" She shook her head for no. "Do you want to tell me what's wrong?"

Daphanie slowly smiled, still looking guilty. "I swore at the teacher. She said I had to go down to the police station and tell them what I said. But I was really scared, so I came down to see you."

Daphanie had grown up with swear words used as nouns, adjectives, verbs and adverbs. Yes, I am talking about the "F" word and the "C" word, among others. Clearly, this teacher was too young and inexperienced to be teaching in the Outback. Imagine sending a child to the police for swearing!

My heart went out to this little girl, so I said, "You were wise to come to me. Good girl. You can stay here. I will tell the teacher I stopped you going to the police. When you return to school, say 'Sorry' to the teacher, and just go and sit down. Have you any other ideas what to do? Anyway, have another ice block while you think."

Daphanie sucked the second ice block. "I think I will say sorry. Then sit down." And off she went to school.

Sergeant B Stories

There were many very good and understanding police who were very fair to the Indigenous people, but one of the new coppers was very odd and mean. I will call him Sergeant B.

Paddy Wagon Terror

Nancy, a very well-respected elderly Martu woman, came screaming into the clinic. "The policeman! He got the little kids in the police wagon! I think he's trying to kill them! He's driving very fast, speeding around the town and I can hear the kids screaming!"

We ran out onto the road and I could hear the terror in the children's screams through the wagon. I stood almost in front of the police vehicle and spread out my arms to force him to stop. He skidded and stopped in a cloud of dust. I ran to the back of the paddy wagon and opened the back of the truck. There were four children, all under the age of five! The tears, the fear, the terror on those little faces will stay in my mind forever. I took them into the clinic and gave them water. They were in severe shock. There were no seats in the paddy wagon; the children were too small to hang on to the wire cage that covered the interior, which meant they had been bouncing around and hitting the metal sides and floor of the truck with every turn and bump. How cruel can you be!

Sergeant B stepped out of the vehicle and asserted, "I will cure these kids for life about graffiti. I wanted to give them a good fright."

Graffiti indeed! I found out later that the children had scribbled on a white-coloured board in the park that served as an outdoor movie screen. Bear in mind that these children were barely tall enough to reach the bottom of the screen. Moreover, their tiny scribbles were barely the size of a postage stamp! Graffiti was unknown to the illiterate locals - let alone tiny preschoolers!

Friday Night at the Pub

Everyone came to the pub on a Friday night. The white section was packed when Sergeant B walked in and bought a slab [30 in a box] of beer. He paid for his beer, pulled down his pants and mooned the crowd. There it was: a large, fat, white bum for all to see. Then he farted and said, "That's what I think of youse!"

He pulled up his pants, put the slab of beer on his shoulder and walked out. There was total silence and shock and then we almost roared the tin roof off the pub with laughter.

Over My Dead Body

I went on a routine visit to check on an elderly white couple in their seventies. As the old man opened the door, I could see that his wife was severely breathless, sweating and had loss of colour. Within two minutes she went into cardiac arrest. We both tried CPR but she died.

I went back into town to ring the RFDS to notify them of a death. The woman had pathology as long as your arm and the doctor was not surprised. He said that he would write the death certificate.

While I was still talking to the doctor, Sergeant B walked into my house, without knocking or calling out. He started to tell me off: "You have no authority to touch that dead body. Dead bodies belong to me."

The husband of the deceased was the Justice of the Peace. He had rung the police to tell them about his wife's death.

"I have every right," I said. "I am the only medical person here."

"When did you last read the *Police Gazette*? I'm going to report you! How do you think you will feel standing before the coroner? What will you say then?"

"It won't bother me," I answered. "I can't wait to tell them about you. Please go."

The sergeant returned 15 minutes later - again entering my house without permission. He tried to kiss me around my lower neck and hug me! He said, "I am so sorry, I got it wrong. I rang my inspector and he said you have authority to do what you did."

I pushed him off me and told him to leave my house.

Trina and the Christian Revival

A group of Indigenous Christian Elders came to our town and knocked on my door. They were really old, old Aboriginal men, and they were wonderful. They said that they were going to have a Christian revival because the Nullagine people were the drunkies, the dropouts. They did everything that was wrong - aunties sleeping with their nephews and so on. To remedy this, they were going to stop the local mob from drinking alcohol.

"We're gonna come out in two-week's time and have this big revival. We'll have this big mob with us and we're gonna *save* them. Save their *souls*. Everyone said to come to you."

They asked if I would drive people down to the Garden Pool where they would all pray and sing. They said, "We know it will work because it stopped us from drinking alcohol."

Garden Pool was part of the Nullagine River, where the water always stayed after the rains, even during the drought. At this point in time, however, it was almost dry. There was actually grass there. The dry, grassy bed was surrounded by wonderfully wide white snappy gums, which were hundreds of years old. When I arrived in the truck with the first load of our Indigenous mob, I noticed that there was a huge bonfire. There must have been about four hundred Aboriginals from elsewhere already at the site. I did three more trips in my truck bringing the rest of the Nullagine mob to the site.

The meeting started and there was singing and praising the Lord in English and their Aboriginal language. The Elders then urged the Nullagine people to confess their sins. Some people stood up and confessed that they had stolen things from my house such as money, watches, expensive sunglasses and perfume! They then began begging Jesus to forgive them.

"I took $50 from Philla's house! Forgive me, Lord!" shouted Elma and then she flopped on the ground.

Rebecca stood up. "I took Philla's perfume and watch. And she thought Trina took it! Praise you, Jesus!" She too dropped on the ground.

Not to be outdone, Big Wilma staggered up and declared, "I took so many things from Philla's house, I can't remember them all!" She then fell to the ground with a resounding thud.

I sat there with my mouth open in astonishment. I was always missing things, and the locals would say to me, it was the Jigalong mob or other mobs. I think the Christian Elders were also astonished. They were expecting confessions regarding their drinking and sins of fornication against the tribal way. Meanwhile, the Nullagine mob was trying to please the Christians by declaring their wrongdoings. I noticed these thieves weren't asking *me* for forgiveness!

Then the Elders said they wanted someone to give testimony, to give witness: "We want someone to stand up and tell their story". I was the only white person there. I was sitting down next to Vera and Trina (who was drunk, as usual). Trina shot up and said, "You want *us* to tell you a fucken story?"

The women around us immediately whispered, "Trina, get down! Get down! You bring shame on us! You bring shame! Vera, get her down!"

Trina was undaunted. She raised her arm and pointed her finger back and forth at the leaders and admonished them:

"You call yourselves fucken Christians! You cunts! I stood at the hotel when youse came into town. I waved to you! I called out greetings! And you *fuckers*, all of you – big truckloads of you -" she said pointing at the Elders, "you *fuckers* turned your heads the other way and ignored me!" Trina flicked her head to demonstrate their behaviour towards her. "And you call yourselves Christians! You've been raving on about 'love one another'. Youse wouldn't even look at me!" Trina was drunk and feisty. "Youse didn't give me the little hand wave!" She repeated herself and re-enacted her waving at the Christians and how they had turned their heads the other way.

Some of the women near Trina were tugging at her dress, trying to stop her and to pull her back to the ground. They whispered, "Trina, sit down. You bring shame on us! Sit down!"

Meanwhile, I whispered, "Give it to them Trina! Get into them!"

And with my encouragement she became more fired up and started to point her finger at them, calling them hypocrites, saying to them that they should have waved back to her, and they could have smiled and not ignored her. "You could have smiled! You hypocrites!" Trina was ripe. She deserved an Academy Award! She continued on:

"You think youse Jesus people! You think JESUS would do that to a poor old drunk woman like me? You think that JESUS would do that?" Then Trina answered her own question: "No! Jesus would say, 'I *love* you, Trina'. But all youse did was blip!" And she tossed her head to the side.

I have to laugh when I recall this event. Trina used the foulest language! (I've edited it severely here). Between every syllable she cursed! Oh, how I wanted to record her!

"God loves you, Trina." I whispered. "God's happy you're doing this!"

The other women chided me, "Philla, you just like

her! You stop it! These good people! These bible people!"
Eventually, three women got hold of Trina and pulled her
down. She landed on top of us!

There was a long silence. Remember, there were
hundreds of people there so the silence was deafening! All
eyes were on us. Then, one of the Elders spoke:

"This is true, what our sister has said to us. Jesus
doesn't want us to ignore these people. This is who we
come for! We've come for the likes of Trina!"

People started to clap and to sing very loudly, praising
the Lord. The revival ended pretty quickly after that. (The
whole event was about four hours long). About thirty
people came over to Trina and put their arms around her
and sobbed. "We sorry, Trina." They laid hands on her and
wailed. Someone said, "We pray the Holy Spirit gonna be
on Trina!" and the group hugged and wailed some more.

This went on for a long time. It was too much for me. I
had to ferry kids and mothers back to Nullagine. I noticed
that the Christians weren't helping too many people with
transport. Meanwhile, the group continued to kiss and hug
Trina saying they were sorry. Everybody (Christians and
locals alike) was crying.

Incredibly (and I do mean *incredibly*), Trina stayed off
the booze for six weeks after that. In fact, so many people
from Nullagine stopped drinking that the local publican
was worried. He started giving *free* meals to entice people
back to his establishment. Eventually, they all returned to
their routines and heavy drinking.

Down in the Pits

Nullagine was founded by a gold rush at the turn of the 20th Century. When I lived there, there were a couple of mining companies and lots of one- and two-man shows out in the scrub.

I got a call from one of the big mines that a fellow had fallen about 300 feet. They thought he was dead, but others said they didn't think he was dead. I had recently completed a course in resuscitation in Perth so I was feeling up to the task. I packed my medical bag because I was *sure* I could save this person.

As I was leaving, the police came out and said, "We'll follow you. But whatever you do, drive slowly. Don't speed. If he's dead, he's dead. Don't kill yourself or have an accident."

The officer knew what he was talking about. There were too many vehicle accidents because people would drive too fast over the sandy mounds and spinifex. They drove 4WDs but overestimated their driving abilities.

"Go slow," he repeated. "I'll go have breakfast, but I'll be out there."

It was a good 60 kilometres to get out there. It was so rough one can't go over 80 k's, so I went slowly. When I arrived, they brought me to the mine shaft. They had this big iron drum that was attached by chains and cables. I went to step into this large bucket and a man grabbed hold of me and pulled me back.

"You don't jump into it!" he told me.

I said, "Well, I'm going to jump into it because I'll feel safer."

"No, you don't jump into it. You stand on the sides," he instructed.

So, I stood on the side and hung on to two chains. Two other men stood on the drum as well. I said, "I think I'd be better in the middle."

But they said, "No, you'll throw it out [of balance]."

This line manager (I think that's what he was) was shaking so much, the bucket was hitting the sides of the shaft as we descended! We had to go down a couple of thousand feet and when we got to the bottom I asked, "Where is he?"

At that moment two fellas came down a nearby ladder and one of them said, "I've never seen a dead person before."

Ever optimistic, I replied, "He's probably not even dead! If you've never seen a dead person, how would you know?"

With that, he got hold of my shoulders and started shaking me backwards and forwards. "Don't you talk to me like that! I've been mining all my life, and if I see somebody's dead, I know he's dead!" He was strong, and as he shook me my head was flopping like a rag doll's - back and forth, back and forth.

Then one of the other men grabbed him. And the manager who was shaking before really started to go spastic. His arms and legs were slackening. I turned to one of the composed men and said,

"Listen! You've got to take this one upstairs because he looks like he's fitting. And take this cranky fellow with you."

Cranky started to protest so I raised my voice and asserted: "I'm *not* having you with me! I'm telling the police on you! The police are probably waiting at the top and I'm reporting you!"

He just lost it completely after that. Bloody men! I get so annoyed when they go to pieces!

One person, whom I'll call Derek, stayed with me. He showed me the ladder I had to climb. It went up about 300 feet. This was mad! Of course I had sandals on and my medical bag was heavy (it contained a couple of drips as well as the usual medical supplies). I got Derek to carry my bag and up, up I climbed.

When we got up there, Derek explained that there was a hole that someone hadn't covered properly. His fellow workers all said that the man was drunk when he came on the night shift. And he walked straight down into the hole. That hole had a drop that was far more than a few hundred feet. When I got to him, it was like his whole face had been sliced off. It was horrendous. It was *really* grotesque. I touched him and his body was cold, like he had been dead a week or a fortnight because it's so cold down there. All I could do was bandage his face so they could transport the body.

I thought it was difficult to climb up the 300-foot ladder, but the hard part was going back down. I couldn't believe it. I kept thinking, 'Oh, this is really hard for me!' My sandals weren't right for going down those rails.

Anyhow, I got down the ladder and took the bucket back up. Sure enough, the police were there. They had to take all the bandages off because they had to photograph everything. I heard that it all went to court.

The Lebanese Doctor

In Nullagine, the hotel pub was the focal point of the town. It's where folks could get grog as well as prepared meals. Eventually, I would go down on Friday nights and socialise. They'd have an iced tea or lemon drink waiting for me.

I ran the dart competitions as well as those for pool and table tennis. A couple of the miners and I became friends and they would come up to the clinic and invite me to go over to play a game. I'd say:

"You go over to the pub, and I'll come over at lunchtime. I'll play you for $20."

Of course, they'd be drunk by then so I didn't have to be very good at table tennis. If they won, I'd pay up.

On one occasion a Lebanese doctor came with our regular Flying Doctor to the clinic. It was hot, as usual, and the Lebanese doctor was asked to go over to the pub to get us some refreshments. It was just across the road and near midday, so it wasn't peak hour. We waited and waited for his return.

After 20 minutes, the Flying Doctor said, "Go over. I think he missed the pub."

"He *can't* miss the pub. That's all there is. There's nothing else in town!"

I went over and walked into the white's section. I looked across the bar and saw the Lebanese doctor standing on the other side. I went out and entered the blackfellas' side of the bar.

"What are you doing in here?" I asked him.

The bartender immediately said, "Phil, do you want something?"

The Lebanese doctor turned to me and asked, "What have you got that I haven't?"

The bartender said, "Is he with you?"

And I said, "Yes, he's Lebanese." His skin was dark.

"I've been calling out, 'Three lemonades!'" the doctor said.

"I thought you were Abbo," explained the bartender.

Stolen Children Reunion

In my early days of working with Aboriginals, there were two elderly sisters who always sat together on the ground, under a tree. In those days there were no houses. They camped in humpies and cooked outside. When I would visit the camp, we gave the usual greetings, "Where are you from?" Then, as I was leaving, I always asked, "Is there anything special I can do for you?"

They would always give the same reply: "Find my

daughter!" Then they would both laugh. It took about six months before I even understood their reply. It sounded like one word - they said it so quickly.

Once I understood what they were saying, I asked, "What do you mean, 'Find my daughter'?"

Coming from Sydney in the 1940s, no one in my area talked about the stolen generation. The sisters explained to me that *their* little girl had been taken. Both the aunty and the natural mother deeply felt her absence. Over the years, they asked every doctor who visited them. Any sort of government person that came along, they asked the same thing. These two old girls would have been well into their sixties by this point.

For years and years, they cried. Now they said, "We laugh at people who ask, what can I do to help you?" (It should be noted that documentation of Indigenous births in Western Australia only started in the 1970s). Years passed and the sisters never tired of the same request whenever I said, "Is there anything I can do for you?"

"Yair. Find my daughter!"

The day came when I was told that I was to have a new boss who was Indigenous. Let's call her Clare. Clare rang and said she was going to look up relatives, and thought that they were in my little town. No name was given. She sounded vague and mysterious to me on the phone.

What Clare didn't know was that the local police constable had come down to the clinic and said, "Your boss is looking for you. She rang me on the phone and asked me if you did any work! She couldn't get you on the

phone. I assured her you were the busiest person in town."
He was laughing that the Director of Nursing would call the
police to check up on me. As far as the Health Department
was concerned, I was paid to work five eight-hour shifts
per week. They assumed that I should be in the clinic and
available to answer the phone during working hours. Yeah,
right.

Then one day Clare arrived unexpectedly in her
capacity as my new boss. She asked about the two sisters
and where she could find them. I offered to show her
where their camp was, but Clare insisted she would go
there alone. No fuss. No questioning me. Clare was away
for about 40 minutes. Returning, she walked into the clinic
and started asking me about statistics and my workload
- just as any manager would. When there was no more
to say about work, I asked directly, "Did you find your
relatives?"

Clare turned and in a detached manner said, "They
were sitting in the dirt! They kept saying, 'Sit down'. There
was no chair for me to sit! How could I sit in that dust?"
She was indignant. And she was surprised how dirty their
clothes were. "They even looked dirty! I am shocked by
how they live."

Staring at her in amazement, I realised this had not
gone as she had planned, or even imagined. With that,
Clare announced she was going.

When I went to the camp to visit Clare's relatives the
next day, her mother said "Too long. Many years gone.
She don't know me. Maybe my daughter. Maybe not. She

no sit down with us. Nothing to say. No want to stay with us. She no cry. Nothin! She just shoved money in my hand. Then gone."

Clare only stayed six weeks in the job. Reason for leaving: She could not cope with the hot climate. She returned to work in one of our capital cities. I found out later that Clare had been fostered by a Melbourne family when she was about seven. She went to university and acquired a degree in nursing. Then she married a wealthy man who lived in Rose Bay, Sydney.

A year later, Clare's daughter, Tessa, arrived. Tessa was doing a story on the stolen generation. Tessa visited me in the clinic. We stood looking out onto the street. In the middle of the road, two very drunk young Aboriginal girls were fighting physically and using very foul language with each other. I could see the horror on Tessa's face.

I said, "Don't judge them. But look at those girls and know *you* [Tessa] could have been one of them today."

She turned with tears in her eyes and answered softly, "I know."

Tessa only stayed one day. I hope she visited the aunties (grandmother and great-aunt). But who knows? No one told me.

Swabs Were Not Enough

I saw a lot of child sexual abuse in the Outback. I'd be called out in the middle of the night. Often, they were children who were intellectually disabled. Very disabled, in fact. I remember doing swabs and trying to be as gentle as possible. Because I believe that if you make a big fuss, it's the worst thing you can do.

Like I said, it happened many times, often in the middle of the night. Suzie's story comes to mind. I remember the women were in the clinic room with me while I was taking swabs. I would sing a little song and I got her to actually laugh while I was taking them.

The next morning, I went down to the police and told them I had taken these swabs. But they said, "You should have called us."

At 2 o'clock in the morning? I should call them? "I don't see what you could do about it," I objected.

They wouldn't accept the swabs as evidence because, as they explained, *anybody* could have gotten into the clinic.

I said, "The clinic was locked all night. It was secure! I had keys and I had locked it!"

"Somebody could have jumped in through the window," they argued.

"But the window wasn't smashed! The window was locked!" I was getting heated.

No matter what I said, the police said no, that the evidence would not hold in court so they would not take the swabs off me.

Suzie had a lot of repair work done. I think she underwent three surgeries. I knew one of the nurses in the Hedland Hospital. She told me that when they put the child into the bath, all the faeces just came way. The rapist had penetrated her bowel. I think for a trauma like that, the child should have gone down to the Royal Perth Hospital. I thought that was a scandal, the way she was treated. Even the nurses were saying she should have been treated by more specialists - pediatrics and that type of surgery. Poor little girl.

Then I made some inquiries because she had come up from Jigalong. There had been other occasions where men had taken her. She was a repeated victim. Suzie was a very simple child. She had just started puberty. She had those little breasts. She was very childlike. When we got her out of the truck, she looked around and held out her hand and said (in her tribal language), "Oh, it's raining!"

And I said, "Yes!" and we both stood there with our mouths open to catch the raindrops. I tried to be gentle; to convey this is no big deal. The women were excited and I said we must be quiet and not add to the trauma.

Bush Medicine

The Martu always came to me to drive them whenever they wanted to get out of town. Sometimes the women wanted to get away from drinking and/or their store credit had run out. So, they would go bush for a couple of weeks. When I was too tired or busy to drive them, they would soften my heartstrings by coming to the clinic with a child on their hip and explain, "We've got no funcken tucker now! You gotta take us!"

I knew they were telling the truth. The store would definitely cut them off when their credit was maxed out. And their credit regularly maxed out. By going bush these desert people could survive off the land while waiting for their next pension cheque.

To entice me to be their chauffeur, the women would offer me the opportunity to know more about bush medicine and where they could collect it. They would only take their swags, a tin of flour, tea and about four tin cups (no matter how many people were going). The most important items were two empty flour tins, one with the bottom entirely cut out. This was their tool for extracting water from a seemingly dry river bed.

We would go to various places, always starting from the Ant Hill Road. They would direct me offroad and point out birds and paperbark trees because they indicated signs of water. The women always knew where to camp. As soon as we arrived in a dry river bed, they would dig a deep hole in the sand and place the bottomless flour tin in it. Over the course of several hours, this tin would fill with water. That provided their drinking water; it was naturally filtered and ready to drink. They drank copious cups of black tea and lived on damper. The Martu hunted goannas and kangaroos, but they did not feed emu to small children because "Emu have too much fat. Make them sick," they explained.

The old women with their sore knees would bury their legs in the hot river sand. After an hour they would feel well enough to go back to town.

One of the most impressive uses of bush medicine happened when I was unable to treat a two-year-old child with impetigo (severe small sores). Antibiotics had no effect. "You need to treat this child with bush medicine," I was told. The women picked leaves and sticks from a special bush and boiled them in one of the empty flour tins. Then they made a hole in the sand and lined it with a black plastic bag, making a small bath. They carefully strained the liquid into this makeshift bath. When the water cooled, they sat the child in it. This child was covered with multiple pustules yet within two days from when I saw her, her skin was completely healed! They achieved something in a few hours that I had tried (and failed) to do over six weeks. This particular medicine from this special bush did not grow everywhere; there were only two places they knew of.

These desert people had a profound knowledge of the bush - both its deadly and healing powers. Small children, as young as four, could point out which vegetation was poisonous and which was edible. They even warned me not to even touch certain flowers because I could rub my fingers on my lips or eyes and poison myself that way.

When they were ready to return to town after their two-week hiatus, they would send up a smoke signal. Someone in town would see the smoke and tell me it was time to bring them back. One important thing to remember is that the local gold prospectors also set fires in the spinifex to ward off snakes. I don't know how the Indigenous knew the difference, but they could correctly discern the differences in various types of smoke.

Skinned Alive

One evening I was working in the clinic when Julie, an Indigenous woman, rushed in and screamed, "Those fucken coppers! I want to sue them! I want a lawyer! I'm taking them to court over this!" Her eyes were bulging in fury.

I didn't know this woman or where she was from, but my psychiatric nursing experience kicked in, and I noted that she was about 30 years old and morbidly obese. She had been drinking but she wasn't "full drunk". She had no skin on her left arm and her left cheek looked badly grazed. Her hip was showing where her dress was torn and her skin was missing there, and her left leg was also red raw. My first thought was that she had been burnt - by fire or hot water? When I took her into the light, I realised her skin had been scraped off - not burned!

"How did this happen?" I asked calmly.

"Don't change the subject!" she yelled. "I want to sue the police! You're just like them! You really don't care about me."

"Oh, right-o. We'll sue the coppers," I said to placate her. "That sounds good. Tell me, what did the police do to you?"

"They put me in the back of the paddy wagon. There was no seats. Nothing to hang on to! And I flew out the back door. And he didn't even stop to pick me up!"

Indeed, Nullagine's paddy wagon was a 'bare bones' truck. Passengers were sitting on metal, with nothing to help them stabilize themselves when the vehicle turned a corner or hit a pothole. Moreover, I knew this policeman, Sergeant B. His idea was to drive fast so that he could scare detainees by tossing them around. He did this with people of all ages, from small children to adults. They were his victims, not just his prisoners.

I gave Julie a cold drink of water and phoned the RFDS. They said they would come straight away. As I put the phone down, in walked Sergeant B with a large padlock in his hand. "I want you to look at this lock," he said to me. "See how when you insert it, it doesn't stay in. Look!" He demonstrated how the lock opened and he repeated explaining to me how the lock wasn't working properly.

Julie screamed at him, "You didn't even stop! And I'm going to sue you!"

Sergeant B didn't acknowledge her. To diffuse the situation, I took him outside. He again demonstrated how the padlock had failed and then he said, "I didn't even know she was gone until I got back to the police station. I didn't know I'd lost her. It's not my fault. This lock should have held the doors closed." He added, "I went back [about a kilometre] looking for her, but I couldn't find her."

"Go and write your report and say all that you want to say," I advised. It was all I could do to control my temper.

When I went back into the clinic, I gave Julie some morphine to control the pain until the RFDS came and flew her away. That was the last I heard of it.

Cemetery Cleanup

A couple of years after her 18-month-old baby died, Margaret wanted to mark his grave. At that time, none of the Indigenous graves were marked.

Both whites and Aboriginals were interred in the local cemetery. Although they were not segregated, their graves were markedly different. The whitefellas usually had a concrete slab over the grave and a headstone to identify the person interred. Poor whites and Indigenous graves, on the other hand, were only marked by a mound of stones. (Think of old western movies of Tombstone, Arizona, where graves were marked by piles of rocks and simple wooden crosses. Nullagine cemetery was like that). By law, there should be a white stick with a number on it. The Shire was required to keep a record of each grave. However, in Nullagine, the sticks had fallen over and many had rotted into the ground. White ants did the rest.

"It costs a lot of money," I cautioned. "What were you thinking of?"

Margaret proposed getting a large rock to serve as a headstone, "You know, like the white men do," she explained. She wanted writing - who was the mother, who was the father, and the lifespan of the baby.

I explained that I could send away and get a brass plaque with all those things written on it. "It will cost about $50." She agreed to pay it.

This was a great idea and it inspired me to think more broadly about some of the others buried there. I went to the young Aboriginal boys who were hanging about the town and said I wanted to get some stones for the cemetery "to mark your people's graves".

Six of them immediately jumped into my truck and said, "We'll show you where to go."

We drove about five kilometres out of town, then off road for another kilometre. To my astonishment, we could see a mountain of slate, many were naturally sliced into thick slabs that were about one by two metres, with lovely coloured stripes running through the stones. We picked up three (they were extremely heavy) and we took them back to the jail. I explained to the senior constable (one of the good coppers), that we were going to start marking the Indigenous graves and I wanted the prisoners to write information about the deceased person on each slab. I also asked him if I could take the prisoners at 5 PM, when it wasn't so hot, to clean up the cemetery. I was surprised by his encouragement. "Yeah, good thinking! You'll supervise them, won't you?"

Both men and women prisoners enthusiastically

volunteered for this daunting task. The cemetery had *never* been cared for. It was surrounded by a broken-down wire fence and an old rusty gate that lay on its side. The grounds were covered with dead, long grass and spinifex. Trees that had once been planted by whitefellas were now only little black stumps. They weren't able to survive the heat and drought so there was no shade whatsoever.

At 5pm I collected a half-dozen prisoners and drove them to the cemetery. I had a few shovels and a hoe, which weren't enough tools to go round. Those without tools pulled out the grass with their hands and put it in piles. "We need more rakes!" some of them said. "You work for the government. You can get that!"

"I've got no more rakes. Go and ask the cops for more rakes," I replied. And they did.

Aboriginals are often criticized for being lazy and indifferent, but I discovered how wrong this assumption is. I didn't need to give any directions. They were very respectful of the dead and they worked solidly for about six weeks, each evening until it was too dark to continue.

Early on, I made the mistake of calling out to one of the workers, "Nancy's buried there. Did you know that?"

Several people immediately put their fingers to their lips and one came over and whispered in my ear, "No talking here. You'll disturb the dead."

Later I discovered that they were very aware of the spirits of their relatives. There were other rituals that I started noticing during the cleanup. One involved smoke, another was the replacement of the rocks on each grave (a task that only the women performed).

I managed to get some white paint and brushes via the pilot of the RFDS. Through the police, I gave them to the prisoners. Their only request was for more slabs to write on. I left the inscriptions entirely up to them. Their phonetic spellings and ways of expressing themselves were charming and authentic. It came from their hearts.

It took a lot of time and a lot of hard work to clear the cemetery. "We did a good job, you know." The prisoners took pride in their accomplishment. The spirits would know that their people had taken good care of them.

Nearly Choked to Death

A long time after her terrible bashing, Cathy returned to Nullagine. I only learned about this when she came into the clinic with a baby that was about nine months old. Her right arm was plastered and in a sling. In her hands she had plastic bags, which contained her shopping. She asked me for a ride back to the reserve.

"I cannot manage the baby and the stores. My arm is paining," she explained.

"Yes, of course I'll help," I replied. "What happened to the arm?"

Cathy told me that she had gone to another town to live and to get away from Jason. However, he came looking for her and they had reconciled. "And now we're back together again," she explained. "Another fight. He broke my arm." All this was said calmly. No anger. No resentment.

When we arrived at the reserve, Jason was standing in the middle of the dirt road, outside his house. He looked menacing. I could see he was not going to move, so I slowly came to a stop. He put his hands on the bull bar of my truck. Looking at Cathy and in an angry tone, he said, "Why did you go to the shop? I wanted something! You didn't ask me! You don't think of me!" He had wanted cigarettes.

Cathy looked frightened. "He's really angry with me," she said.

Despite the time gap since I last saw Jason, I clearly remembered the brutal bashing that almost cost Cathy her life. The police had been notified. So, what, if anything, had happened about that? And now Cathy has a broken arm and he's complaining about her shopping without consulting him! Enough!

I sprang out of the truck and stood with my hands on my hips. "Why has Cathy got to do *your* shopping? Aren't you a strong man? You lazy drunkard!" This time he was going to get a piece of *my* mind. "You bashed this woman! Now you've broken her arm. What will you do to Cathy now? Break the arm that's already broken? Is that all you're good at?"

With that, he turned around. He took his hands off the bull bar and proceeded to put his large hands around my throat and strangle me. "You don't tell *me* what to do. She *my* woman!"

Cathy put her baby on the floor of the truck and it immediately started screaming. She jumped from the vehicle and pleaded, "Stop! Jason, stop!" as she tried to get between us.

I had gone down on my knees, gasping for breath. I was fading fast and my vision was blurred. Cathy had taken her arm out of the sling and was pulling at his fingers, trying to loosen his grip on my throat. It helped. A little air got in.

"She a white woman!" Cathy warned, "They hang you, Jason, if you kill a white woman! Let her go!"

Did Cathy do something to his fingers? Or was it something she said? I don't know, but Jason let go and I fell in the dust. Although I went down in a heap, I got up as fast as any bouncing ball. I jumped into the truck. Cathy too was in the truck like a shot. The baby was still on the floor screaming. Jason put his hands back on the bull bar, standing defiantly.

I wanted to kill him! All the abuse of men towards women that I had seen for years gathered inside of me like a volcano! Unless you have experienced *real anger*, there is no way can you relate to the above phrase. I put my foot on the clutch and revved the engine, ready to drive over the top of him. Cathy threw the gear stick into reverse and shouted, "Don't do it!"

My foot was already on the clutch so when I let it go, we reversed at the speed of light. I turned the truck around and I drove straight to the pub, where I knew I could find the police. I blasted my horn, and he walked straight out to us.

"What's happened?" he asked cautiously.
"Look at my neck!" I insisted. It was very red. "Jason tried to strangle me! Look at the marks on my throat!"

The officer walked around the vehicle to Cathy and said, "You have to get away from Jason. He will kill you. It's just a matter of time. He *will* kill you! Look how he has attacked Philla!"

No sooner were the words out of his mouth when a road train crept into town. Because it was turning the corner, the truck was travelling very slowly. The police put up his hand to stop the driver. We watched them speaking with one another. When he returned, he said to Cathy, "This man will take you to another town north. Some of your people are there. Do *not* return here *ever*. Cathy, Jason *will* eventually kill you."

With the help of the police, Cathy climbed aboard the truck and headed north with her crying baby, her broken arm, and her plastic bags of stores.

Olive: "I Blind Bugger"

Olive was a very old Martu woman. She spoke five tribal languages, never washed, and had no respect for whitefellas. For more than fifty years she lived with a genuine Afghani who was born in Kabul and arrived in Australia as a small child. As a young man he walked with the camel train. In contrast to Olive, he was gentle and respectful.

Olive's greeting to a new person was always the same: "I blind bugger." In one year, over a million people go blind in the world with a treatable disease known as trachoma. Flies, poor hygiene, and untreated conjunctivitis meant that trachoma was rife in our Indigenous communities. Doctor Fred Hollows was the first medic to visit the Indigenous people, to set up yearly examinations in order to eradicate trachoma. In subsequent years the team was led by an ophthalmologist from Perth. This eye specialist usually came twice a year. His team would identify problems and recommend corrective surgery in Port Hedland. As a community nurse, I was involved in aftercare, ensuring patients' eyes were bathed and eye drops were applied every day following surgery.

For two years I constantly tried to encourage Olive to have her eyes operated on. But Olive was not a compliant nor grateful client. When I tried to talk with her, she would pull her eyelids down, open her mouth and make faces. She thought that was hilarious. Despite this, three different times I attempted to prepare her for travel to Port Hedland, I'd give her breakfast, get her showered, and find clean clothes for her to wear. This was not easy for Olive who was a true Indigenous desert woman. Each time I drove her to the airport so that the RFDS could fly her to the Hospital, she would go no further than the airfield. Olive enjoyed sitting in the truck so we would get that far. But, no! She would *not* get on the plane. No way, no how!

However, Olive had a dear friend, Nettie, who lived in Jigalong. Olive found out by the bush telegraph that Nettie was very sick and had been admitted to Port Hedland Hospital. Olive came to me and said, "You gotta take me to see Nettie. She wants to see me."

I knew the local police were going to Port Hedland that day, and they agreed to take her to see Nettie.

As fate would have it, Olive was walking through the hospital, when a visiting eye specialist from Perth approached her. By some miracle, they convinced Olive to let him help her. Following her operation, the Flying Doctors brought her home. When she got off the plane, Olive walked over to me. She kissed me all over my face and hugged me. Saying at the same time, "I didn't know. I didn't know. I not know you can make blind people see." Olive kept kissing me all over, crying with happiness.

From that point on Olive no longer greeted people with, "I blind bugger." Instead, she would call out, "I can see you! I see you!" And I could tell that she was truly grateful.

Suicide Prevention

The children were very good at telling me whenever people were sick. I can recall Daphanie coming to see me one day with a group of little kids. Breathless and puffing she said, "You know that whitefella over there? He got a gun in his mouth!"

We all ran to find this man. When I got there, the whitefella was sitting on the veranda with a shotgun between his knees and the barrel near his mouth. The children all came up on the veranda with me.

He shouted, "Get rid of those kids!"

I said to him, "These children have saved your life!"

I turned to the children and asked, "Do you want to leave?"

With their little open mouths, they shook their heads slowly sideways. "No, we want to stay."

"Well, here we are. You can't kill yourself in front of the children. Best to give the gun to me," I said firmly but gently. To my surprise, he handed me the gun. I unloaded it and handed the bullets to the kids. I helped the man to his feet. The children, the man and I walked very slowly to the clinic.

Daphanie said to me, "Here's the bullets. We goin' now."

This was a great success story because within a few hours, the RFDS sent a plane and flew the man out for treatment. He returned three months later, a completely different person and a recovering alcoholic.

Nabaroo: He Too Far Gone!

One night in 1988 at about midnight I had a phone call from the Roebourne Prison. I told the warden that I thought that he had dialled the wrong number.

He asked, "Are you Phil or Philla?"

I replied, "Yes."

"Well," he said, "that is who we want to talk to regarding Nabaroo. He wants to kill himself."

"Well, you need the psychiatrist," I said. "You need medication. You need a suicide watch. You don't need me! I'm 500 kilometres away!"

"No. None of that is possible," said the warden. "We have no doctor on call. We are not allowed to give prescribed medicines. The Aboriginal boys here in jail said Nabaroo must talk to you, and you will make him better."

I argued my case further, again saying that they needed to get professional help for him *there* at the prison. Then without further ado, the warden announced, "I'm putting him on the phone now!"

I knew that Nabaroo was a diagnosed and a well-documented psychotic young Aboriginal man about 19 years old. I said some kind words of comfort to Nabaroo on the phone and spoke to him about all of his family members, calling them by their Indigenous names and relationship to him. I was saying words that I thought that his relatives would say to him. I spoke to him of how we all loved him, and that we cried because he was not with us; how we waited to have a party to welcome him on his return to his home to Nullagine where he belonged.

The only two words I heard from him were 'Hello' at the beginning of the phone call, and 'Yair' as I concluded the call. What happened to Nabaroo in prison in relation to his mental condition during and after that 20-minute conversation I will never know.

After he was released from prison, he returned to Nullagine. It was not long after his return that another serious mental health episode occurred. The Aboriginal people from the camp went to the local police station and spoke to the police. They were very concerned because Nabaroo was handling knives and he was threatening people.

The police came to my clinic and told me that they would not put him in jail because of his high suicide risk. At that time in the 1980s, the rate of Aboriginal deaths in custody was very high. In Western Australia, for example, approximately 16 Indigenous prisoners had hung themselves in jail. All sorts of terrible accusations were made against the police. Common sense should make us ask, why would the police put them in jail to kill them? There were cameras, witnesses. I never believed any of the wild stories that flew around about the police.

I rang the RFDS in Port Hedland and they prescribed some calming medications for me to administer. They said that they would come to Nullagine the next day to fly him to the Perth mental hospital.

Meanwhile, I asked Nabaroo (the name that he was known by within the Aboriginal community) what he wanted now, and what he would like me to do until the plane arrived.

"I want the *Mabin Man* [Indigenous medicine man]," he replied. "And to sleep at your house."

My heart almost stopped. This would not be easy. Nevertheless, I put three mattresses outside, in my unfenced large backyard. I went to the Indigenous camp and found the *Mabin Man*. I told him how the police had refused to put Nabaroo in jail because of his suicide risk and about the arrangements I had made with the RFDS. I also said that Nabaroo wanted the *Mabin Man* to sleep in my back garden with us.

The *Mabin Man* stared at me and said, "Philla, he will fucken kill me first! Then he will fucken kill you! Not good! He too far gone!"

The three of us eventually settled down on the mattresses outside. The night temperature was about 28° C. I had a syringe loaded with sedation medication under my pillow in case Nabaroo became agitated or violent. My dog (a dingo named Ping) slept very close to me. I was exhausted and went to sleep in less than a minute. I don't know how long I slept. My dog woke me with a very low, serious growl.

I could see the *Mabin Man* dragging his mattress away from Nabaroo. I lay very still. After about five minutes Nabaroo moved his mattress up near the *Mabin Man* again. This manoeuvre between Nabaroo and the *Mabin Man* was repeated about three times. Ping kept waking me with his soft growl each time they moved. I was pleased that Nabaroo and the *Mabin Man* were moving further away from me. 'That is good,' I said to myself. 'It will give me a better chance to run away if Nabaroo tries to come towards me to kill me.' Sleep eventually came to me.

Ping growled again. It was just on daylight. The *Mabin Man* was gone! Nabaroo was standing up looking around. The medication that I had given him prior to us settling down to sleep was intended to give him a good sleep, so hopefully it had done that.

I rose from my mattress and said, "Time for cup of tea, Nabaroo."

He followed me slowly into my kitchen. As I put on the jug, I saw him open the knife drawer and start to take the knives out. "No, my darling," I said, "I need those to make the breakfast with." He handed the knives to me. Breakfast was brief and then we left my house and we walked over to the clinic.

Then to my great relief, Nabaroo wandered off across the road towards the store knowing full well it would not open for several hours. Thankfully time is not an issue to the Indigenous people like it is to Caucasians. Nabaroo was prepared to sit and wait outside the store. Eventually, the RFDS aircraft arrived from Port Hedland to fly Nabaroo to Perth. There were two police on the plane along with a nurse and a doctor. Two police escorted me and Nabaroo to the unsealed airstrip situated in bushland.

After being all night in the open with Nabaroo it was shocking to see how many police and health staff were required to escort him to the mental hospital in Perth. I had his family with me to say farewell. The plane flew off in a great cloud of dust. The desert women stood and cried.

Two weeks later Trina, his mother, said, "You ring and find out where my son is."

Ringing Mental Health in Perth, I was told Nabaroo had run away. No one had notified anyone.

Rock Concert

Like me, the police had to cover a lot of territory. We were at least 120 kilometres away from the next clinic or police station. Once a month our local police would go out to the Aboriginal camps and talk with various communities about any problems they had. It happened that on one such occasion, I was home when an Indigenous woman came to get me.

She was laughing when she came to my door and said, "You got to come down. There's a rock concert on. A *big* rock concert on! You *got* to come with me!"

I said, "Oh, I don't want to go to a concert."

"Come!" She was insistent.

I relented and went with her down the hill. As we got closer, I could see a crowd but no band. It turned out there were about a dozen white people in the hotel and about forty Aboriginals throwing rocks at the building. Rock concert. I get it. The little kids were running down to the creek and bringing back more stones. They were having a great time.

For some reason, the publican had shut the door to the hotel and wouldn't allow the Aboriginals to enter. This made them angry. They probably wanted to go in and sit where it was cool. Of course, drinking might have been a motivation as well. I don't know the full story as to *why* the publican wouldn't allow their entry. No doubt he had his reasons.

Then things got serious and the crowd started to smash

the whitefellas' 4-wheel drives. Well, a 4WD is your *life* out there because it was the only means of going anywhere to get food or anything!

As this started to happen, along came Trina. (I don't know where she came from). Full of the confidence that alcohol provides, she decided that she could talk her way into the hotel. But as she approached the doors, somebody threw a rock. It hit her in the head and she went down. The men inside the hotel heard her fall and they said it was just like a big watermelon being thrown down! Two or three of the white men came out of the hotel just as I got to Trina. She lay on the ground with her head split open.

I just stood up and said aloud, "Look, I think you've killed Trina! Now you've got to stop. She's dead! Now stop. Stop! Stop the stoning!"

And with that everyone dropped the stones. And then they all just sat down. I knew she wasn't dead. At this stage, I was half wishing she was. I'm no saint! She was good and cute most of the time. But she neglected her kids. She did dreadful things to the kids.

They asked, "Is she dead? Do you think she's dead?"

"No, she'll never die, this one. Whether she's dead or not, we've got to pick her up."

Just then Trina opened her eyes and called, "Philla! Philla!"

Well, it was the whitefellas that picked her up and carried her to my truck. I needed to dress her wound, contact the RFDS and have Trina taken to hospital.

"Why don't one of those black bastards come and help us?" one man complained.

"Look, don't think about it," I cautioned. "You'll get more stones thrown."

Then they started to ask, where were the cops? I told them they were patrolling other camps. Clearly, in remote locations like Nullagine, the police cannot be everywhere all the time. But I'm sure things would not have gotten out of control if they had been in town. It helped me to appreciate the moderating effects of a police presence. Hopefully, the next rock concert in Nullagine will feature music.

Mistaken Identity

One time I took a little Aboriginal girl (Cindy) to the Cardiac Unit at Port Hedland Hospital for some tests. She was about five or six years old, small and skinny. A little slip of a thing. She was scared but they didn't want me to come in with her while they performed some tests. I asked, "Why not?" and the clinical nurse explained that the doctor thought he could handle her better if she was on her own. I stupidly listened to them.

When Cindy came out of the examining room, she leapt on me and wrapped herself around me like a monkey - her arms and legs enfolded me. I asked her how it went and she said it was awful. They had put needles in her and she was frightened.

Then the nurse came out and said they had used quite a

few needles, but they hadn't worked. They wanted Cindy to go in again. The little girl clung to me again and cried, "No! No!".

So, I said to the clinical nurse, "No, you had one go at her."

"It's not good enough," she insisted, "We want to do another test."

"No, you're not," I said firmly.

"You can't talk to me like that!" the nurse chided.

"I just did, Darling. I just did," I pointed out.

The conversation went on like this, with the nurse saying the doctor said this, the doctor wants that.

"You've got to do what the doctor said," she asserted.

"I don't care if the *Pope* said it," I replied, "This little girl is frightened. She's scared!"

"Well, you can come back in with her," the nurse said.

At this point little Cindy was hanging on so tight, she was practically strangling me.

"She is terrified. And I am *not* subjecting this child to any more trauma. It's as simple as that." I said this slowly and firmly to convey that I meant business.

"You'll have to come back again!" the nurse persisted.

"Well, there you are. The problem's solved." I agreed facetiously.

"I didn't mean *that*. Come in now. You've got to come in *now*," the nurse insisted.

I raised my palm like a stop sign to silence her. And I said, "I'm going now. That will be the quickest way. We won't fight anymore."

With that, Cindy and I walked out of the hospital and made our way to the Community Health Department, which was down the hill from the hospital.

When I entered the transportable building, the nurses were all there, sitting at their desks doing paperwork. They all knew me by this point so they looked up and greeted me. I couldn't wait to tell them what happened!

"I just had a go at that bloody sister [nurse] up there."

I recounted how Cindy was so frightened and how they wanted to put that little child back in for more needles. Then I added,

"I couldn't believe the way she spoke to me! She spoke to me like I was *nothing*!" With that, everyone started to laugh! I asked them what were they all laughing about.

"Have you looked in the mirror lately?" one of my co-workers asked.

"What do I have to look in the mirror for?" I replied.

"Look at you!" they answered, "Your hair is full of red dust. You're as brown as a berry. They probably thought you were the girl's mother, to start off with. You're *terribly* black, Phil. And look: you're dirty!"

I looked down at myself. I was wearing my usual fawn-coloured shirt and brown culottes. "I'm not dirty! That's just dust!" I argued, "This is a clean shirt. I put it on fresh this morning." As I said this, I patted my shoulders and stomach and all this dust came billowing up! You see, I had just driven over 320 kilometres on dirt roads from Nullagine at some ridiculous time - four o'clock in the morning. I couldn't deny that I was dusty.

The nurses kept laughing and laughing at my Pig-Pen impersonation. But then one of them pointed out, "That nurse would have thought that you were Cindy's mother."

"Do you mean to tell me that she would speak to ... Wouldn't she speak *kindly* to me if I was the mother?" I asked. My question was genuine.

"Oh, for sure. She thought she had the upper hand. And that's all there was to it. If the doctor [the cardiac specialist] finds out that you're a community health nurse, and you're the one from Nullagine, there will be hell to pay."

The doctors really did respect me. But why wouldn't they give the same respect to the little patients and their parents?

Indigenous Funerals

Funerals were considered important. The Martu told me that it was a big insult to the family if you did not come. But you might not always know the deceased. Maybe you were related through Lore, or the tribal way. Perhaps the connection was through someone who knew them. It's easy to make a mistake.

Besides missing a funeral, there is another problem, a very *big* problem. In Indigenous culture, immense blaming takes place. Fights break out at funerals because the deceased wasn't looked after well enough. For example, maybe a woman died of cancer in the Royal Perth Hospital but she was somebody's Auntie, and they should have looked after her better. So: bash, bash, bash! The Indigenous believe that things happen for a reason, which means someone must be responsible. Payback, revenge, and punishment are deeply embedded in the Indigenous way of life. Anyway, you can see the potential for conflict.

Our town averaged *at least* one funeral a month, and hundreds of Aboriginals from all around would come to the cemetery. Police were always in attendance, and it was common for 10-12 officers to turn up to control any fighting. They always seemed to know when fights at the grave were going to break out, which was quite often, and they knew when to bring extra police. There were times when the Elders would go to the police to tell them they expected trouble. I found the police were excellent at funerals. They would settle fights quickly and quietly - no arrests or shouting.

From the onset, I showed my respect by attending each and every funeral in Nullagine. There was no hospital or morgue locally so the hearse would come from Port Hedland (or rarely Newman) and go directly to the police station. Usually around 8am, the undertaker, police and Elders would start the funeral procession from there. The Indigenous would load up on the back of trucks or any available vehicles and follow. Others would wait at the cemetery gates.

I gradually learned about the strict cultural protocols associated with Indigenous burials. As they took the coffin out of the hearse, everyone would follow into the cemetery. The women would all start to scream and cry. This could go on for 10 to 15 minutes. It was common for the police to go over to the presiding Elder and say, "You better get going. It's very hot." It *was* hot and bound to get even hotter. Moreover, it would take hours for the backup police to get back to Marble Bar and Newman.

"Give them a minute. They'll settle. Just wait," the Elder would say. He would never just start talking. Expressions of grief were expected and respected.

The police always thought they ran the funerals, but the Aboriginal people knew that I would be there and see that everything went right. The women would show their grief by wailing, rocking back and forth, and bashing their forehead with a stone. The old girls, in particular, would keep going till they had blood running down their face. They did this to show their deep, deep mourning, their *real* sorrow.

Anyone who was related (by blood, Lore, or tribe) was not allowed to stop their self-harming. So, in the middle of their wailing and rocking someone would whisper my name to get my attention and they would give me the eye. It was my cue to intervene! I had to fight them for the rock. They wouldn't just hand it over. There would be fisticuffs as I tried to pull the stone away. Some women were real fighters. On these occasions, a couple of the young boys would come over and hold her arms while I pulled the stone out of her hand.

I became involved in this ritual by accident. I had

previously worked in a psychiatric ward for the criminally insane where patients would self-destruct like you wouldn't believe. (Besides, it is only common sense to stop someone who is self-harming). Early on, however, I was unaware of these cultural protocols.

One particular day the sun was belting down on us and it was very hot. I was feeling really tired and I didn't feel like getting involved. As a former nun, I would go into a little bit of ecstasy saying prayers for the dead in Latin. I thought that was more important than stopping people from hitting themselves. And I thought, maybe they want to hit themselves. Then one of the mourners who was rocking and wailing hissed my name and gave me a look that conveyed it was time for me to do something.

The Aboriginals always assumed that because I liked and accepted them, I should know all these things. I remember in my third year at Nullagine, Wilma admonished me:

"You didn't stop that old lady!"

"I didn't want to interfere with your way, with-"

"It's your job!" she exclaimed.

"It's *my* job?" I didn't get it.

"Yes! You got to stop them. That's *your* job!" Wilma reiterated.

I got this flash of insight. Ahhh! After that, I would always reassure the old ladies by saying, "Lots of *midgie midgie*!" [Blood]. In reality, there might be just a little bit of blood on their temple, but I would try to let them think they had drawn lots of blood. They would nod their understanding and let me have their rock.

The grave would be prepared and the coffin lowered. Once the Elder had spoken (in their tribal language) attendees were expected to shovel dirt into the grave. Again, no one related to the deceased could do this. They would send out messages to other tribes to come in and bury them. Sometimes only a few people would rock up. I would pitch in and shovel some of the dirt. I was quite good at it and I often persisted beyond the three or four shovelfuls that were normally expected of any individual.

The police never stopped the self-harming mourners nor did they shovel dirt into the grave. They would only act once the blaming began ("It's all your fault!" someone would shout) and the men would start fighting. As I mentioned earlier, the police were very good at curtailing conflict.

Funerals normally came to an end with the women covering the grave with rocks. However, there were a few times when the men would line up in twos and make their way down to the river bed. As they went, they would shuffle their feet as though performing a little dance. They would take small branches from nearby gum trees and flick them above their heads as they chanted and circled near the shoreline. Someone once told me they were letting the spirit [of the deceased] go. There may be more things but that is all I know.

Tobias and the Good Copper

I had been up since 5am working in the clinic and had come home for lunch about 2:30pm. I was tired and starving. I had just finished cooking one chop, one potato and one carrot when Tobias knocked at my door and said he was hungry.

Tobias did look very hungry. He had been drinking heavily and there had been a fight. He had been punched in the mouth and his lower lip hung down to his chin. It was still bleeding. I felt so sorry for him that I gave him my precious dinner. He gobbled it down in less than 30 seconds. Once he left, I realised that I should have offered him half of the meal because I too was so hungry. I sat at my table tired, dejected, regretful and famished!

There was a bang on the door yet again. I opened it and to my surprise, there was a white man from the gold mines standing there. He had a plate of hot food in his hands that he had bought at the pub. On the plate was a pork chop, chips, pumpkin and cabbage. He told me that he had come into Nullagine for a late lunch. He had ordered two meals and had told the cook that he was going to take one of them to the nurse because she was always working so hard. This kind gesture was like a gift from heaven for me because I did not actually know this man.

The next day I went to see the police, one of the 'good' coppers (he was exceptional, actually) that I worked with and who had the desert people's welfare at heart. I asked him if he could help me: I was worried that Tobias' lip would not heal if he continued to drink and get into fights. If it did not heal, he would have to be flown to Royal Perth Hospital for surgery. The police officer suggested that Tobias could be placed in the jail until his lip healed. We both explained this to Tobias telling him that going into the lockup would help his lip to heal and it would protect him from further injuries by preventing him from drinking and fighting. The officer also explained that Tobias would be a free man and be able to walk to the store every day. Tobias was happy at the suggestion that jail would be his safe home for the next few weeks and that he would be able to come and go as he pleased.

The jail provided basic accommodation. It opened at 6am and closed at 8pm and during the day the prisoners (all Indigenous) were allowed to sit outside the compound, but they were never permitted to walk further than the broken-down waist-level wire fence that led to the road. Despite the lack of security, no prisoners ever tried to escape, or even cross the line.

There was an old open wood stove outside the cells where they could cook. The police often took Indigenous prisoners out in the police wagon and the police would shoot kangaroos so that the inmates would have kangaroo meat to eat. The prisoners were allowed to operate the spotlights to see the kangaroos at night but they were never allowed to use the guns.

Tobias' lip healed very well to the surprise of everyone, even the doctors. He did not have to go to Royal Perth Hospital for surgery. Tobias was so happy - he felt much better and that he could eat and talk properly again.

A year later some Indigenous children came to tell me that Tobias was locked in the toilet and asked if I could go with them to get him out. I spoke to the police telling them about Tobias' dilemma then we all went to the Aboriginal reserve to get him out of the toilet. The toilet door could not be opened so a boy was put onto the policeman's shoulders so that the child could get into the toilet through the opening at the top of the door and then unlock the door from the inside. When the boy got into the toilet and opened the door, we saw that poor Tobias was dead. He was only 47 years old.

Isabel in Labour

I was down at the Aboriginal reserve doing my early morning call-up of the children, and I noticed a pregnant lady, Isabel, who was from Jigalong. She was standing outside her house and leaning on a post. I was in the truck transporting the little ones and their lunches to school, but gave her a long stare as I passed slowly by. Isabel made no wave or even eye contact so I assumed she was okay.

I was inside the school and was placing the lunches in the fridge when one of the older boys who walked to school ran in puffing. "Quick, Philla, baby coming now! You gotta hurry now! Jigalong lady!"

I jumped into the truck and raced the one kilometre to the reserve. Yes, it was the lady who had been standing by the post. Isabel was a big woman and I wasn't sure I could get her into the truck so I asked her if she thought she could get herself in. She managed to lift herself up and as I took her to the clinic, I tried to assure her by saying calmly, "I am here. I will look after you."

No other words were spoken. Her breathing was heavy, but controlled. I could see she was in advanced labour. As we walked the 12 metres from the truck to the clinic, Isabel had to stop several times due to contractions. She was amazingly stoic and practised her breathing to control her pain. None of the usual - no drama, no shouting, no anger or cursing at me. Isabel was a remarkably strong, self-controlled woman.

When we finally entered the clinic, I asked Isabel if she thought she could manage to sit on the bed. She shook her head no. I lifted her dress quickly and there was the baby's head. I said as kindly and as compassionately as I could, "Could you drop to the floor?" I threw a flimsy sheet and pillow down as I took her weight and we both eased down.

At that moment, in ran Nancy, an old Indigenous lady who would normally assist with births. "I help ya!" she said. How on earth did she know we needed her help? Despite living in the Outback for so many years I could never figure out how the local Aboriginals were able to communicate so quickly and effectively. Yes, there were always people sitting under a tree or hanging outside the store so maybe they gave the word. But for me, it has always been a mystery.

I told Nancy I needed something to cut the cord. To

my horror, she promptly went outside! I thought she had come to help! Meanwhile, the baby's head was crowning and Isabel was puffing heavily. I tried to steady its head so it would not come too quickly, else the baby would have a headache. I found another sheet. Within a nanosecond, I just had time to catch the baby and stop his head from hitting the floor.

Not a cry or a complaint from Isabel – other than a deep grunt as the baby left her womb. Using the bed sheet, I handed the baby immediately to the mother. I had to draw up the drug we give quickly after birth to help safely remove the placenta. With that, in walked Nancy. "I been lookin for a sharp stone. Couldn't find one. But here." She handed me a broken beer bottle!

"What is that for?" I asked incredulously.

"To cut the cord! That's what you told me to get."

Nancy then gave her full attention to the baby and the mother while I went and collected the silver box, which contained maternity equipment, from the nursing trolley.

The cord was left on longer than usual, but it does give a blood transfusion to the child. There was certainly a big mess of amniotic fluid and blood on the floor. I threw lots of paper bed roll and forced myself to ignore the bloody mess.

Nancy and I got Isabel up onto the bed and helped her into a sitting position. I asked her why did she not call me when I drove past her on my way to the school earlier.

"I saw you very busy with the kids," Isabel explained. Imagine: Although she had been in the second (and painful) stage of labour, she had put the children's going to school first. What a wonderful, strong woman!

Pub Apartheid

During my first six years in the Pilbara, there had been no rain. Not a drop! I invited the Indigenous people to come to the clinic to shower and wash their clothes. After all, encouraging good hygiene is an integral part of community nursing, in my view. After a while, people became more and more comfortable being in the clinic and talking with me. At times it felt more like a hang-out than a nursing post, which meant I was privy to a wide range of their conversations and concerns.

Normally they (mainly the women) would walk into the clinic and out of the blue they would start a conversation. For example, one woman burst into the clinic and announced,

"This is wrong! We should be able to walk into that bar! What's so special?"

The pub practised racial segregation. There were two entrances: one for whites and one for blacks. Inside, the bar was L-shaped and it served to divide the two sections. Patrons could see and call to one another if they chose to. The whitefellas' section had stools along the bar as well as all the amenities of the hotel. There was a restaurant with tables and chairs, and a recreation area (featuring a pool table and a ping pong table). By contrast, the blackfellas' section had two big barrels. That was it. There was no seating or games room. When it was crowded, the barrels were used to hold drinks. Aboriginals had to practice patience after they called out for service because they were served last.

It was like playing the lotto. Some of the Indigenous women never tired of sneaking into the white bar. The publican was more tolerant than the barman, and frequently both of them were in the kitchen so no one was guarding the bar. The weather would be extremely hot and these women would be happy with a refreshing lemonade.

The woman who barged into the clinic protested, "I was in the bar and Bill was going to buy me a lemonade and the barman said I had to get out and come in on the other side [the black's entry]. It's *wrong*!" There was real anger about this!

"Of course, of course," I replied, "I think it's wrong too."

And I did feel it was wrong, *extremely* wrong! When I lived in Sydney we were horrified by the South African policy of apartheid. Then I moved to Western Australia and discovered that *we* were separating the blacks from the whites, and I was shocked.

When I heard that the Premier of Western Australia was visiting Marble Bar to hear people's concerns and to help the Aboriginals more, I jumped at it. There were so many indignities, so many injustices that our Indigenous people were suffering needlessly. I thought this was one thing I could do to improve their treatment. I got dressed up (and looked beautiful, I might add) and drove all the way there to talk with him. At a reception, while standing beside him with a cup of tea in my hands I found my opportunity to introduce myself and I started to explain the practice of segregation at the pub in Nullagine.

"You can't talk to me like that," the Premier interrupted.

And I said, "What? Is there protocol for how I should address you?" (Your Eminence, Oh Great One, what?)

"You never come and tell the Premier your problems. You go and tell someone and then they come and talk to the Premier. That's protocol."

"Look," I said, "I've travelled over 120 kilometres just to get here. And I'm here now, and I've got to talk to somebody. Nobody else is talking to you. And there is a black and white bar -"

"I will ask one of my ministers to come and talk to you about it."

Nothing happened for every bit of two years. Two years! Then one day in the clinic the women were jabbering away in their tribal language. It wasn't long before they were fighting and getting more and more angry. English curse words peppered the discussion. All of a sudden, I heard my name being thrown around so I asked,

"What are you talking about?"

"You know," they said. (There was always this 'you know').

"What?" I asked.

"You told the Minister you didn't like the black and

white bar and the man came down and talked to us in the park."

Then another woman added, "It's all your fault, Trina, that they don't want us women in the white bar."

"How can it be Trina's fault?" I asked.

"Remember when the politician came down and asked us? And Trina, you said, 'No, there's no problem.'"

"When did this happen?" I probed.

"Long time ago. We had a meeting in the park. Didn't you see us?"

"No," I said.

"He came down [some 400 km] and he sat in the park with the women and the men and had a meeting for about an hour. And he shouted us all a drink. We said we all the same. We should just mix. But Trina kept being bossy. She kept saying we like it better this way."

I griped, "I went to the Premier to complain! You always said to me, 'Why should there always be a black and a white bar?'"

I was annoyed. Why hadn't I been contacted? And why did they not tell the Minister of Aboriginal Affairs the truth about how they really felt? I had gone to a lot of trouble to support them. Forget annoyed, I felt betrayed!

I knew from previous conversations that some of the young Indigenous men wanted the opportunity to talk to the miners. They thought they could pick up a bit of work if they were allowed in the whitefellas' bar. Some of the women liked to go in and flirt - drinks, romance, the usual bar activities that white women can take for granted.

With the exception of Trina, both the men and the women said they wanted equal access to the bar. But when they started to complain, Trina spoke over them and said, "No, there's no problem."

"How could you? I went and complained about that!" I protested.

The recollection of that day led to more arguing in the clinic. Actually, they were *screaming* at each other. Shouting and cursing, "You fucken cunt!" and all that. Clearly, the issue had not been resolved. Indeed, the injustice of pub segregation resulted in a violent protest at one point (see: Rock Concert). So why did the Minister only listen to one person?

It took some doing, but I finally teased out what happened during this so-called consultation. Participants in the group started to say they didn't like the separation and that it would be better if everyone could mix, but Trina (who was always drunk) talked over them. She accused the women of just wanting to "fuck a whitefella".

"I think we're better drinking with our own. We can laugh and talk our way. We don't have to be with those whitefellas. They're rubbish!" Then Trina added, "The publican feeds my children when I'm really drunk. He always gives them a bit of food. And I'm not going to talk about him when he's so generous."

Then somebody else said, "Oh, you know when things are really bad, the publican will come out and hand the kids some chips or something if they're hungry."

Trina pointed out, "They're all blaming me, but they

could have said something. And when he asked us, 'Are you happy?' everyone kept quiet. Nobody said anything! And when he said, 'I want to know,' everything was quiet. He said, 'Well if you want to leave it like that, we will.'"

When I left the Pilbara in 1996, the bar was still segregated, long after South Africa changed its policy. At present, the Australian Government wants the Indigenous to have a voice in parliament so I think it's important to look deeply into what happened in Nullagine.

I want to point out six (6) things that were problematic. First, the person who made the initial complaint (yours truly) was not included in the consultation. Later I will explain my potential contribution. Second, the "focus group" was selected haphazardly. The Minister of Aboriginal Affairs made the effort to travel all that distance to talk with residents. This was impressive. However, he saw folks sitting under a tree and interviewed only them. How accurate a representation of the population was this?

A third point is that in Nullagine, the adult Aboriginals had little or no formal education. Many did not speak English fluently. The Royal Perth Hospital would have been the furthest they travelled. It is likely they had little perspective about the issue. Does a fish know it's in water? Most locals had only the experience of pub segregation and racism. Some felt the "wrongness" of this division, but how well could they articulate its repercussions? I could have helped out.

The fourth issue concerns culture and group dynamics. I wasn't there so we can only speculate about this.

However, despite the group's majority wanting access to the whitefella's bar, only one person's opinion dominated. Trina was intelligent and adept at arguing. She made good points that hit their target and silenced the other participants. But if we pull back and look at the situation, we can see that one of the heaviest drinkers in town was objecting to access to the whitefella's bar! Why? Gratitude. The publican would feed her children when she was too drunk and couldn't. However, loyalty and gratitude should not be pitted against racial equality.

This leads to the fifth issue. Lack of perspective. Nullagine was a very small town with less than 100 residents at the time. The whole community could have been invited to participate. Views of the bar staff, patrons (blacks and whites), the police, the nurse (me again), and the broader community should have been included. It is important to see the whole picture.

The sixth point I want to make is that the visiting Minister was part Aboriginal. He bought drinks for the people he interviewed that day. Without a doubt, he entered the whitefellas' bar and was served there. If he had also walked into the blackfellas' section, he would have experienced the disparity for himself.

There is a chance that after *all* this proposed effort people would still decide to keep the bars segregated. Maybe. But I would like to think that a proper consultation would lead to positive change. Maybe there would be better communication amongst residents. Maybe the blackfellas' bar would be upgraded to the standard enjoyed by the whites. Or maybe they would compromise by having a "happy hour" so that the bar would be integrated for a specific time period. Any of these potential changes would be better than nothing.

Newman Morgue

This is a serious example of Tribal Lore that took place in Nullagine, where I worked. A man and a woman were married "the wrong way". They were 28 and 30 years old, which meant they were above the age of consent and they made the decision for themselves. Their marriage was in opposition to Tribal Lore. They knew it was considered wrong. As it was explained to me, it was like an aunty and nephew living together as husband and wife. Now, the designation of aunty and nephew is not necessarily due to bloodline, but to kinship - which tribes could marry, which could not. The couple had one child, who was about three years old.

There were many Indigenous reserves in the Outback where no alcohol was allowed. However, Nullagine was a place where they would come to drink, which is why this family came to our town in the first place. Domestic violence was common between this couple. Screaming and smacking each other was routine.

One night, several Martu (including this family) were under the trees drinking into the late hours. Unsurprisingly, a violent, drunken brawl broke out. A very large woman fell onto the sleeping child, and the little girl was killed. She was dead for some time before the police became involved. They were not familiar with this mob from Jigalong, so when the police came to tell me about the death, they also asked me questions. I told them the parents' names, where they were from, and some background information.

There was an investigation and a coroner's report. I do not know whether any charges were laid, and I never heard anything more about that. However, the deceased child was taken a couple of hundred kilometres away to the Newman Morgue, where it stayed for several months. No one came forth to claim the body. Because the parents had broken Lore, I was told, people did not expect the child would have a long life. That was the parents' punishment.

The Aboriginals continued to ignore the request concerning the little girl's burial. The undertaker asked one of my colleagues, who was a community nurse, if she could help to do something to resolve the situation. Pat put the little coffin in the back of her car and took the deceased to the Nullagine cemetery. The undertaker had previously organised the gravediggers and they helped Pat with the coffin.

Now, this is the amazing part of this story: Despite months of nonactivity, despite months of no communication and despite no advanced notice, the Indigenous community gathered near the Nullagine cemetery within minutes of Pat's arrival! Several cars pulled up in a flurry of dust. The parents and relatives stood near the entrance to the graveyard, which was some distance from the gravesite. No one would enter the cemetery itself. As the coffin was lowered into the ground, everyone wailed and cried. They comforted one another, placed their arms around the bereaved parents and they all sobbed together.

After all that time and all that distance, how did they *know* about the exact time and place of burial? I know from living years in the Outback that the Indigenous people can sit and wait and observe for incredible periods of time. I can imagine that although they just appeared to sit around the town, the Aboriginals had constantly watched the morgue, looking for a little coffin. There would always be someone keeping watch. They would know the *minute* the coffin left the morgue. They would have called out to the relatives via "the bush telegraph", jumped into cars and followed my colleague for nearly 200 kilometres from Newman to the Nullagine cemetery.

Although I lived 15 years in close contact, I learnt one thing: Whitefellas (myself included) cannot fully understand the Indigenous way, their thinking, their deep passionate love of country, or the complexity of their culture.

Treatment for Depression

When I was 16 years old, I went to a local First-Aid Course. I was the only girl while the other students were mainly men who worked for the Shire or men who wanted to receive a certificate to assist at local football matches.

I did the six-week course, and I remember the only oral question I had to answer was, "If you were walking down King's Cross on a Saturday night and suddenly someone cut their throat in front of you, what is the first-aid assistance you would think of?" The First-Aid examiner was a doctor.

"Put my hand over his throat?" I answered in a tentative voice.

The doctor corrected me: "Stick your fist into the wound, and hold it there. Then in loud voice call for help to ring emergency!"

Some 40 years later, on one hot day in Nullagine, the Aboriginal children ran into the clinic to get me. "Billy has cut his throat! Blood is spurting!"

Another eight-year-old said that Billy was just outside the clinic. I ran out and saw the jagged top of a tin can that Billy had used to slice this throat. I stuck my fist into his carotid vein and told the children to run to the pub, which was just across the road.

"Tell them I want the police. Anyone, come and help me!" (There were no mobiles in those days). The children did as I requested, but no one came.

Many years before a surgeon had told me when

someone is going to cut their throat intentionally, they throw back their head. By doing so, however, their carotid artery falls *away* from the neck. Thus, they cut a vein but miss the intended artery. So, the chance of survival was good!

All this time with my fist on the wound, Billy was saying, "Let me die. Let me die. I am nothing. I am nobody."

At the pub, because they found out from the children it was an Aboriginal that was bleeding to death, no one from the hotel came to help. But they did phone the police and he arrived quickly. He helped me to take the severely depressed man inside the clinic where further surgical procedures were carried out on the advice from the RFDS. Within 90 minutes Billy was flown away to a hospital.

The senior constable was a compassionate, kind man. In fact, he was one of the best policemen I ever had dealings with. I told him that we need to make Billy feel wanted and respected, that Billy is somebody in the community. We have to be ready for this when he returns.

The senior constable suggested I could have Billy cut my lawn and pay him. However, I decided he could be my assistant for the road accidents or severe traumas I dealt with. I truly needed someone to handle the phone, especially when my hands were busy with a procedure. Billy could talk in several tribal languages. And he could offer reassurance and find out if the patient was willing to go to hospital. (All too often Aboriginals did not want to go away from their community).

When Billy returned to Nullagine, the senior constable and I sat down with him and talked about his problem and how work would help ease his depression. Billy was impressed that we cared. "You're gonna do this for me?" We reassured him that we always liked him and that we really wanted him to work with us.

Billy was given the lawn job immediately. This proved to be a real status booster. He had a job with the police! Within a week, he voluntarily walked into the clinic, washed his hands very well and went over to the cupboard and put on plastic gloves without being told to do so! Billy had heard there had been a fight and he had come to the clinic to help. I began to wonder if Billy was psychic. He would show up at the right time and often did exactly what I needed without my having to tell him! Of course, in a small town like Nullagine, the local Indigenous sat around most of the time, watching and watching. There wasn't much else to do.

Billy flourished. He continued to help at the clinic although it was only the Police Department that gave him a wage. These jobs changed Billy's life completely. Everyone in the community started to praise him. "Billy, you doctor!" they would say. And he would stand more upright. He was also admired because he had a job for the police. There is a theory that work can help alleviate depression. Well, it worked for Billy!

Eve in Custody

When I worked in Nullagine, I lived next door to the jail. On the western side, there were three concrete jail cells with iron bars that led to a common open area. At the opposite end of the building was another concrete block, which contained two toilets and a shower. It was stinky and very dirty, with green moss on the floor. If you have ever had chooks, you can imagine what the central common area looked like. Wide chicken wire served as the roof and walls.

During the day, prisoners were let out at 6am to sit outside the jail walls where they played cards and sang out to their brothers and sisters (not necessarily blood relatives) as they passed by.

One evening, I heard my name being yelled to come quickly. Much screaming, crying and begging me to come *now*! Quick!

The Aboriginal police aide lived opposite me. As I ran down my steps, I could see him coming out of his house at the speed of light. Neither of us asked questions of the other, just trying to use every breath to run faster. The police aide unlocked the gate, as the prisoners shouted to me, "Eve, she hung herself!"

Another gate had to be unlocked. While still looking through the bars, I could see that the scarf Eve had used to hang herself had snapped and she had fallen to the ground. Unconscious or dead? I was not sure. There was obvious cyanosis around her mouth. Her whole face was bulging and turning purple. The aide was unlocking the door and I ordered him, "Go get a sharp knife to cut that cord!"

"You will cut her throat if you cut the cord. I don't think you ought to use a knife!" the police aide argued. He was scared.

"Quick! A knife is the only way I will save her!" I insisted, raising my voice.

"Get the fucken knife!" screamed several of the prisoners. They were upset, and with reason: In their culture, they would be blamed for Eve's death. They could be speared because they should have looked after her better. According to the reasoning of their Indigenous culture, when bad things happened, somebody was to blame; someone should have sat outside her cell and talked to her, looked after her. A few years later, the regulations for incarceration changed so that when Aboriginals were jailed for minor infractions, they were not left on their own.

The Aboriginal police aide ran into the station and quickly returned with a pen knife. "Is this any good?" he asked.

"No! Get a sharper one!" I shouted to be heard above the wailing.

The police aide ran off so while I waited, I used the pen knife to get underneath the cord. I did nick her neck, but at least I could get air to her lungs. CPR followed. Eve gasped. She was back. I wanted to pull Eve outside to get some fresh air but she was a large woman so I needed help. I turned to see where the police aide was. Gone! Where? To tell his boss!

When they finally arrived, the boss (a senior constable) went straight into the Police Station - not into the jail! I asked myself, why would he do that? I later found out that he wanted to sign the papers for Eve's release! When he finally came into the jail, he said, "Eve, you are legally free to leave. No charges laid."

I was dumbfounded. Eve was still in a drunken stupor and still blue in the face. She had no idea what was going on! I was expecting the police to assist me, to show some compassion. Nullagine was a very small place. He would have known her, her history. Why wasn't he offering me help to get her to the clinic? He was following the letter of the law, not the spirit of the law.

"What's going to happen now?" I asked angrily.

"She can go," the senior constable replied.

"She can't walk! Where is she to go to?" I argued. She certainly wasn't mobile. She was in no state to get up and walk!

"That's not my worry," he said. Once she was discharged, his responsibility finished.

"Well, I'll have to take her then," I said, hoping for some acknowledgement and sympathy. After all, I had saved her life. But to no avail. They wanted nothing more to do with Eve in order to avoid any controversy related to death in custody.

Fortunately, several of the inmates helped to put her in my vehicle. I took her to my home so Eve would have a proper bed to lie on and I could nurse her, administer oxygen and notify the Flying Doctors.

You might ask, why would Eve want to commit suicide? She was only in the cell for being drunk. Was it just the grog? Some background information can help us better understand the situation: Eve was only 19 years old, beaten many times and packed raped three times in the past that I knew of. She felt unloved. She drank heavily for years. Life wasn't easy.

The Aboriginal police aide was in a precarious situation. His job was to help the senior constable (his boss), to negotiate with the Aboriginals and to diffuse conflict situations. He had no power, no authority, and he was an outsider. This police aide had a wife and children. His house was provided as part of the job. To qualify, he could not be from the local community. The aides had to walk a thin line between the whitefella and the Indigenous cultures.

It's Important!

Trina staggered into the clinic and asked me if I had time to talk to her. "I have something to say," she announced. "It's important!" She was drunk, as usual.

I replied, "Yes, I have time to listen to you," and I immediately sat down.

She said that she had been to the store, and they had told her to go away because she was just a drunk. Then she went to the police, and they told her to come back tomorrow because she was drunk. Finally, Trina went to the hotel and spoke to the publican to tell him that she had something 'important' to say, but he just ignored her. She knew it was because she was drunk.

Trina complained, "Nobody has time to listen to me! Now you know me, I am *always* drunk! *When* are they going to listen to me?" It was a good point. Nobody wanted to listen to a drunk, and Trina was always drunk. "It's important!" she repeated.

I asked her to tell me what she wanted to talk about. I emphasised that I would sit and listen to her. I began by asking, "What would you like to say?"

Trina began, "You know me. I'm a-l-w-a-y-s drunk!" she said opening her arms expansively. "*When* are people going to stop and listen to me? Never! Fucken never!"

I couldn't help but laugh. "Ah, Trina, that's so true! I do love you, Trina."

"And I love you too, Philla. And when you're dead, I'll still love you!" Then she continued explaining her plight: "Because I am always drunk, I want them to take the money out of the pension. And give the money to the hotel. Then my three children will have a good feed every night." She then explained, "You gotta get permission for that! The money is taken out of the pension. And that's the way they do it."

Trina had obviously done her research. She knew how the system worked and she needed someone to do this for her.

"But no one will listen! I don't like my kids being hungry."

Trina was right. No one took time to listen to her. She was an Aboriginal woman and she was always drunk. But she was intelligent and she was trying to do the right thing for her kids. The storekeeper, the police, the publican - no one stopped and actually listened.

"I will go and see them all, Trina. And they will listen to me," I promised.

Things to Know

A couple of members of the Criminal Investigation Bureau (CIB) from Perth walked into my clinic one morning. After introductions, they asked me would I give a talk about tribal Aboriginals and general information on life in the Outback to the trainees at the Police Academy. I explained that I only passed through the city on my way to catch a plane to somewhere else.

"Anytime you pass through, arrangements will be made to fit you in for a talk to them. Any time between 9am and 4pm." They explained, "The young city cadets have no idea what life is like out there. They need to know how to talk with the Aborigines. All the things that you know, Phil. That's what we want you to tell them."

I did not go. But I will mention some of my experiences with the new local police. I was moving around Nullagine in the Health vehicle. I was doing some dressings on the old ladies. While going up to the school I saw the police car flashing its lights at me. I thought the driver was saying 'good morning' since I was not speeding.

The next time the blue lights flashed, the senior constable spun the wagon across the road in front of me. I jumped out of my vehicle as he did too. "What's up?" I asked.

To my surprise, he answered, "The people in the town tell me you don't like me."

"What people?" I asked.

"The men at the hotel. When we're having a drink together."

"If they said that, I must have said it." I thought a bit more about this, then added, "It's true. I don't like you."

With that, he burst into tears, and asked, "Why? I really want you to like me. Please, tell me how I upset you!"

"Well, you are not fair in dealing with the Aborigines. You don't greet them. You do not answer them when they say good morning. That is what they tell me. Is it true?"

"Will you like me if I say hello to the blacks?"

"Yes, I will like you," I promised.

The policeman didn't seem to realise how much it upset the local Indigenous when their greetings weren't returned. They interpreted his lack of response as showing he didn't like them. It was disrespectful and it was personal.

After my talk with the senior constable, he did improve his interactions with locals. "He got to know us a bit better," they told me.

• • • • •

Another time a truckie walked into the clinic. "How do you live in this terrible place?" he asked in an angry manner. "I've broken down three hundred metres from town. I walked into the police station and asked if he could go and guard my truck while I organized help with my boss. There is over a million dollars' worth of goods on it! The policeman looked at me and *smiled* and asked me if I would like to buy some gold for my wife!"

Indeed, this particular senior constable did spend a great deal of his time collecting and selling gold. The truckie continued, "He bent over and pulled out an old shoe box of gold nuggets. He said to me, 'When you see the gold, you will change your mind. I am sure there is someone you would like to give a gold nugget to.' I was so angry I walked out." The truckie asked me if I had any advice.

"Yes. Go to the pub, there is a phone there. Have a cold drink." I replied. It was hot. His face was red and he was probably dehydrated. The truckie was hesitant. He was afraid locals would steal things while he was gone. "I am *positive* no one will rob your semi-trailer," I assured him. "Everyone in the town has a sleep in this heat for several hours."

I knew the locals wouldn't steal. The tyres wouldn't fit their cars and he wasn't carrying useful items like food or booze. Yes, there were Aboriginals who would steal, but they were selective. They only took things that they could use.

Tragedy

A large Punmu mob (about 500) were practising Lore in Jigalong. On their way back home, they stopped at Nullagine for a funeral. After it was over, there was the usual drinking of beer. The drinking would finish once their money ran out.

The next morning, I was in the clinic when Laura Lee's husband, Donnie, came to say goodbye. They were headed back to Punmu, where they had relocated some time before.

"We're family now," he said to me, "I saved your life!"

It was years ago, but how could I forget? I had accidentally come across a big mob in the bush. They were preparing to do Martu Lore. Secret men's business. The penalty for sharing these secrets was death!

"We all dressed up, our paint and feathers on. The *Kadaitcha Man* put a gun at your head. He thought you were a whitefella spy! He wanted to kill you. He was *real* serious! You remember how I talked to him in our language real fast? I talkin Martu way."

Donnie had assured the *Kadaitcha Man* that I was fair dinkum, I could be trusted, and that I would *never* tell anyone about what I saw. "You very lucky I was there. I spoke up saying you always kind to the Nullagine mob."

I nodded in agreement. While he was defending me to the *Kadaitcha Man*, Donnie had whispered to me in English. He told me to get in my truck, put it in reverse and drive away as fast as I could. Needless to say, I followed his instructions to the letter!

"Yes, I remember it very well. And to this day, I *never* told anyone," I reassured him.

Donnie gave me another hug and laughed saying, "I always look out for you, my sister," and with that, he walked out the door to make the rough 300-kilometre drive (465 km if they used roads) back to Punmu, which was out in the desert.

I remember it was round 10am, when the RFDS rang. "We have just received a message from Punmu. It's a radio call and difficult to understand. The only bit we heard clearly is that a vehicle left Nullagine from a funeral. There was a serious accident and they reckon that nine people are dead." He asked if I knew any of them.

I replied that I knew this mob *extremely* well. I asked what kind of car did they have? When he told me, I burst into tears. "Yes, I do. Donnie Moore is one of them."

"I didn't mean to upset you," the doctor replied. "We are getting ready to fly out there now. When I return, I'll phone you."

It was the biggest call-out the RFDS did up there. It was so tragic, so unnecessary. Eleven people had left in a van. They had been drinking and hadn't taken enough water for emergencies. Unfortunately, their vehicle broke down; it had run out of oil and the engine had seized. One of the men went off to shoot a kangaroo. Its blood would help them to survive. They never found him. Another passenger was a child about 4 years old. He had been in hospital for six to eight months and they were taking him home. The post-mortem showed he was the first to die.

Two girls, aged around 11 and 13 years old, walked across the desert in the searing heat for about 60 kilometres to the base camp to get help. It would have taken them a long time to walk that distance. They were the only survivors.

When the Flying Doctors arrived, they found everyone at the scene had died of thirst. It had rained, but the rain had come too late. The dead were lying in pools of water and scattered all around. Among them was my Martu brother, Donnie, who had saved my life.

· · · · ·

Later on, the two surviving girls came out to where I was living. I could see bruises on their arms and faces. I asked them why they were in Nullagine since their relatives lived elsewhere.

"Everyone was beating us," they explained. "They said we should have taken more water with us."

"But you did!" I said.

"Yes, we did. We took two big canisters [which would be equal to 16 litres easily]. And they told us, 'Well, you didn't take enough and they all died. And that's your fault! You knew they were all drinking, and it's your responsibility! You should have taken more water.'"

The girls remained in Nullagine and did well, as far as I know. Sometime after their visit, I spoke to one of the older Indigenous women about it. She confirmed that particularly being girls they should have looked after everyone. Never mind they were only 11 and 13 years of age! I wish there was some way to stop this dreadful syndrome of blaming and punishment, especially when people are *not* responsible.

Hot Tar Treatment

The bush gang was working on the roads, sealing some potholes in the 200-metre main road of Nullagine. Without warning, the hose they were using burst at a joint, and a worker was splashed with hot tar. You can just imagine the pain! His fellow workers immediately poured cold water over him from the water bottles that everyone constantly travelled with. They called out to me to come and help and I shouted, "Just keep pouring that water!"

We brought him into the clinic and I put him under the cold shower while two of his workmates helped me. We removed his clothes and I asked them how did they deal with it normally when someone gets a splash of tar? They answered that they rub the area with diesel. So, I told them to go and get the diesel and we rubbed his arms. I told them not to go near his face. He had his eyes shut the whole time. In the midst of this chaos, Billy arrived, washed his hands, and put on his gloves without saying a word. He stood waiting for orders. "Call the Flying Doctors for me, Billy, and tell them it's urgent!"

Once Billy got through, he held the phone to my ear while I continued with the diesel treatment. "I have a man covered in hot tar over his face, in front of his body - mainly his arms. I'm having success removing it with diesel," I said.

"Stop using that diesel! You'll make it worse!" the doctor directed.

Since we were having such success with using diesel, I continued the treatment while telling the doctor that I would stop. As the tar came off, we used soap and water to remove the diesel. I then used cream to moisturize his skin. The whole time we kept asking the patient if he was okay and he assured us, "It's good, it's good." I don't know how he managed the pain, the poor fellow! Fortunately, the RFDS was already in the air and close by so they were able to come quickly.

About two years later, the man who had been burnt stopped me in Port Hedland and shook my hand. I didn't recognize him, but then he told me that he was the "Tar Man". To my amazement, he had no scars - not on his face or even his arms! When he was transferred to Royal Perth Hospital, the ophthalmologist had said, "That nurse saved your sight with how she handled your burns." He was truly grateful for my care and expertise. It was nice to hear that he was okay, and that I had made the right decision.

Picking up the Pieces

I remember another mining accident that involved a driller. He was in the hotel the night before, and he told people it was going to be his last shift. It was too hard, too dusty. He planned to go back to Perth. But when he went to work, something happened to his drill. It was just a little hole and he bent over to see better, and something came up and just sliced his head off in a dreadful way.

So, a young constable and I went out to the mine and saw him lying there. I started kicking the dirt to cover the driller's body and the constable said, "What are you doing!"

"I'm burying him. Don't you see there's flies?"

"You can't do that! We've got to pick all that up and give it to the coroner. He weighs it." This was a young bloke, a junior cop.

"I don't think that's right," I said.

He said, "Yes! I'll get into trouble. I rang them up and they told me in Port Hedland that I've got to be sure and get everything. We have to pick it all up and put it in a bag."

I'm so much wiser now than I was then. We had a plastic bag and we started the task. I would reach for something, close my eyes and turn my head away. Then I'd peek for a second, pick up something else and drop it in the bag. After doing this about three times, I thought, 'This is mad! Why are you doing this madness?' I turned around and opened my eyes and there was the bloody cop walking away!

I called out, "Hey! Where are you going?"

"I have to talk to the men. They're all down at the shed. And they'll explain to me what's happened," he answered.

"You're supposed to be here!" I declared.

"No," he argued, "it's *my duty* to find out what happened."

Later someone told me he just couldn't stomach it. It was too much for him; all he wanted to do was vomit. He put in his report that he didn't want to vomit on the evidence so he left it to the nurse to collect!

You know, when I first arrived at the scene and I walked up to the driller, all I could see was these beautiful boots and socks, and beautiful young, brown legs. He was probably in his twenties. It really had the impact of a young life that was taken much too soon.

Violence and Aboriginal Women

Many nurses often said to me when we attended extra training sessions, "What do you do out there in the Outback? You can't be as busy as town nurses."

"I save lives," was my permanent answer.

I went to many, many car accidents. More than I can recall. But when it comes to saving the lives of Indigenous women, I remember each event - vividly.

I once came across four men kicking an Aboriginal woman. She was curled up on the ground as I was driving past in the health vehicle. "Stop!" I shouted as I rolled down the window. They did not even miss a kick - let alone look up at me. "You will kill her!" I warned. They gave no acknowledgement of my presence. I could see they were in a drunken rage.

I jumped out of the truck. On the ground nearby lay a star picket. It was made of iron for fencing. I picked it up and hit two men across their backs. They went down with a plop. The others stopped to look at the situation. They were very drunk indeed. I grabbed the girl, put her in my truck and drove off.

She warned me, "They will hit you for that."

I thought to myself, I would rather be in the hospital with fractures than know that I had left a helpless woman on her own with four men kicking her to death.

Another time I was called to the jail by the police. A visiting lover had stabbed a female inmate numerous times. As I arrived the policeman was running from his home with a couple of towels towards the jail.

"What are you doing with the towels?" I asked.

"She's really bleeding!" he explained.

There were already two towels drenched in blood on the floor beside the victim. Yes, I was able to save her. But the perpetrator said to me, "I'm her husband. I can do these things. She unfaithful!" Imagine: standing there in the jail, and he still felt *entitled* to take her life!

I remember another occasion, like so many, where I was called to a home on the reserve and a woman was lying helplessly on the ground. Her assailant would tell me he had the *right* to punish her. What made it more disheartening was that the other men who were present cast their eyes to the floor and nodded in agreement.

According to statistics provided by the Western Australian Government, Aboriginal women are 32 times more likely than non-Aboriginal women to be hospitalized from family violence. I don't know how they calculate this because women can be raped and bashed by tribal members as well.

Little more than a century ago, white women and children were considered property and subject to violence without protection from the judicial system. As far as I can tell, Indigenous girls and women are still unprotected. As a nurse, I have treated young girls, tiny children (even babies) as well as grown women who had been sexually violated. No charges were ever laid. And there was never any tribal "payback" either.

Indigenous women also participate in bashing other women. For example, two young girls were beaten because they were held responsible when drunk men neglected to put oil in their vehicle before heading off in the desert (see: Tragedy). How can or should Australian law deal with this?

The most important question is, what *can* the Australian judicial system do when violence (spearing, bashing, and payback killings) is considered a prerogative of Aboriginal culture? At present, we seem to do nothing. Surely, we can do better than that!

The Blackfella Doctor

One day every fortnight the RFDS came to my clinic to provide consultations to the people in our region. On one of their visits, they brought a young African-American medical student to experience the Outback. As we drove from the airport into town, the Indigenous ladies spotted him. I could see the surprise on their faces as we drove by. Seconds after we entered the clinic, these same women arrived breathlessly.

"Could we see that blackfella doctor?" They had run to the clinic (in the blazing heat) as fast as we could drive!

I went into the doctor's office and I told the visiting student that the local women wanted to speak with him.

"Not me! I'm a medical student, they really don't want me," he insisted.

The senior doctor urged him, "Yes, you go and talk to them." So, he came into the waiting room with me.

Before I could do any introductions, Milly asked, on behalf of the others, "Do you know Michael Jackson's mummy?"

The student was dumbfounded. Absolutely stunned, he turned to me and whispered softly, "Is she for real?"

"Yes, they are very serious," I answered.

I started to laugh but Milly was undaunted and sailed on. "You do know Michael Jackson!" she insisted.

"I know *of* him, but I don't know where he lives. I'm from New York!" the student clarified.

This was meaningless to the local Aboriginals. At that

time, they had no TV, no radio or magazines. Their sense of country was tribal and based on kinship. Whenever they encountered a stranger, they would ask, "What country are you from?", which meant Indigenous boundaries that marked various tribes within Australia. Distances between California's Neverland and New York City meant nothing. Milly continued, "We want you to tell Michael's mummy: we all listen and love his music. Now you tell his mummy, Michael not allowed to do that to his skin. Being black is good!"

The other women all chorused, "Yeah, black good. Black like you!"

The student pulled back in shock. The women were barefoot, their hair was dusty and their clothes were ragged. By contrast, he wore a pressed white shirt, dress pants, socks and shiny shoes. For the Indigenous, there was no class distinction. They just wanted him to know: 'We black, that's good. Now take that message back to your country.' Then, oblivious to his reaction, they added, "If you don't see his mummy, then tell Michael." With that they shook his hand and said "We love Michael Jackson's music." Satisfied that they said their piece, they left the clinic.

The student seemed dazed. He went into the consulting room and sat down and shook his head. "What happened out there, Phil?" asked the Flying Doctor.

"They wanted him to take a message back to Michael Jackson's mother." I answered while laughing.

"I thought it wouldn't be medical," chuckled the doctor.

Over lunch, we teased the student about getting the message back to Michael's mum. Till this point, he was dead serious. "I don't know Michael Jackson! I don't know where he lives!" The student assumed the women were making fun of him.

To reassure him that the women were serious, we explained that the women wouldn't have had any clue where America was.

"I'll tell you a story of what they did to me," I said, "to give you some idea of their lack of world geography: One night at 2am, a group of Aborigine men knocked on my door. They told me that war was coming to Nullagine." Both men leaned forward because I tend to speak softly. "At first I thought there was a war between the tribes. But actually, they had just heard about the Gulf War on the radio and they thought it was in the Timor Sea area. They told me that they would look after me and take me to a secret location in the desert to keep me safe. 'Give us plenty of notice when they're coming with the guns,' they told me."

The American student finally laughed. He realised the women were sincere and not trying to put him down. "This will be a good story when I get back to the U.S.!" he chuckled.

The Love of Samuel and Helen

Helen and Samuel were truly lovers. They were in their thirties and both were heavy drinkers. But unlike so many of their compatriots, there were never any incidents of domestic violence. Now, Samuel committed a criminal act. I think that it was probably related to stealing. It must have been more than just breaking into the pub for some grog because he was taken up to the Broome jail in the Kimberley region.

Unknown to the police, there was a certain section in that jail where prisoners could communicate through the wall to someone standing outside the prison. It was a common way for the Aboriginals to carry messages to each other.

His darling Helen took herself off to Broome to talk to Samuel through the wall, so he would not miss her too much! This was no small feat because Broome was nearly 750 kilometres away and she had no means of transport. Moreover, her legs had been crushed in an accident some years before so walking wouldn't have been easy. Most likely she hitchhiked from one roadhouse to another, from Nullagine to Port Hedland and then to Broome.

Samuel had a lovers' talk with her until about 6:30 in the evening. At 10 o'clock the same night the police found Helen's body in the scrub outside of the town. She had been murdered. They took Samuel out to the scrub to identify her, which he did. They told Samuel that if he had not been locked up at the time, he would have been the main suspect.

Samuel told me that when he looked at Helen's dead face, he knew he would never drink again and that he would do everything to become a Christian. He would work to change other Indigenous men from ruining their lives with the 'drink'. Many times, Samuel would ring me for a chat. I always said to him "Come back, Samuel, and help me here in the Pilbara."

"No, no," he always said. "Too much temptation there. I ain't strong enough yet." However, true to his promise, Samuel did persevere in preaching the Good News to his Aboriginal people and he stayed sober.

No one ever found out who murdered Helen - or why.

Under Surveillance

I was putting the children's clothes out to dry at the school one day when a strange thing happened. The clothesline was behind the washroom and toilets. No one could see me from the front gate. The time was about 7am. I had four children showering. Suddenly, an army jeep with two army boys came racing around the corner. They had to brake hard because they would have hit me. Their faces had a surprised look. I don't know who was more startled - them or me! They immediately put the jeep into reverse and disappeared as quickly as they had come. They must have thought there was a road here, I thought to myself.

I returned to the reserve for more school children. I

noticed that the army jeep was parked in the scrub. Later when I returned to the clinic, I saw the same jeep parked in a lane near the pub. They were watching me!

I had just parked my vehicle when in a cloud of dust, the health inspector barreled into town and stopped beside me. "Will you have a cup of tea?" I offered. He had just driven 120 kilometres and he would have benefited from a stretch.

"No! Get in the car!" he said. "We'll go straight out to the mine now." He had previously made an arrangement with me to check the water at the mine, which was about 60 kilometres away. But I had no idea he would come so early.

When I got in his car, I told him that I was sure the army was watching me. He replied that I had been in the Outback too long and that living on your own makes you think these things. Now we were on a deserted dusty road, no houses, no trees, only spinifex and scattered hills. We were more than 20 kilometres out of town when an army helicopter appeared over the hill.

"Look I told you the army is following me!" I insisted.

The Health Inspector looked at the helicopter and said, "They have binoculars on us. They are certainly watching us because there is nothing else around here!"

There were several more episodes of helicopters, binoculars and jeeps, but the telling of this story is to remind you to *be careful whom you talk to*. I wrote and mentioned these incidents to a male friend in Sydney. Two years later he was in a bar in Oxford Street, and he struck up a conversation with a fellow patron who told him how he had been with the SAS doing military exercises in the Outback. My friend asked him what type of things do they do out there. He answered that they had been assigned to follow a person for eight hours and to report back with every detail of their comings and goings. As part of their surveillance exercise, they were supposed to find out personal things about this person - in this case, me!

The SAS guy couldn't believe that one person could fill in the day with such constant activity. They wondered if the sergeant had informed this person (me) to give them the runaround as they couldn't believe that anyone could have such a hectic schedule. My friend remembered that he had heard this story before and asked the SAS guy if he remembered the name of the person and he said, "Yes, Philomena."

My friend never let on to the SAS guy that I was a good friend of his. But how news can travel! This verified that my suspicions weren't imagined from being in isolation in the Outback. I felt vindicated.

Astral Travel

When I had holidays, I frequently went to Paris because I had a niece there. I talked to some doctors who came to dinner one night who did astral travelling. I was asking them for all sorts of details, but after 20 minutes they looked at me and said, "Why are you asking us all these questions? You work with Aborigines! They're the people who astral travel. They've been doing this for thousands of years. Go home and talk to them!"

When I came back to work, I saw this old *Mabin Man* who had quite a reputation for appearing, or should I say visiting, people in hospital in Perth and telling them someone had died, or some tragic news. It was mainly about tragic news. I approached him and said, "They tell me that without getting on a bus or car that you can go to Perth and talk to people and communicate with them."

He looked at me very seriously and said, "Yes."

And I said, "But you a drunk man! Seven days a week you're drunk!"

Without taking offence he explained, "Well, it's like you have a nice hankie and you washed it, and you put it in a drawer and you kept it clean. You leave it there a long time and then you open the drawer and the hankie's clean. That's with me." He continued, "When I'm gonna do something, I sober up. It's like pulling out the hankie and I use that power."

I asked, "Could you teach me that?"

"Oh," he replied sadly, "No. You too busy running around too much. You no good."

"Well, if you got something and you can't teach it, I don't think you got it," I challenged.

"If you was serious," he replied, "I'd take you out, way out in the desert. Sit you quiet there for three months ... or with you, maybe six months. Just quiet and just eating.

183

Just look at the birds, get really still. *Then*, I might be able to teach you how you can sit in your mind and go and visit people and tell them messages."

I asked, "Is it always tragedies?"

"No, sometimes I go visit people who have gone down [to Perth] because they're sick and they're just real lonely. And I go there and tell them we're at home and that we're thinking about them."

I have known Aboriginals who were over in Perth, which was about 1,400 kilometres away, who came and told me news that they had known about because the *Mabin Man* had come and told them. It was a very well-known fact among the Indigenous that they did have power with the mind. I believed this man. I believe there were many of these old Aboriginals who did have this power. They could just sit very still and visit someone in their mind in a telepathic way.

I remember asking one of the young fellows, did he understand about using his mind to travel? He said, "Ah, yes, but you got to sit still under the tree a long time and get very quiet and still before you can do that. You can't just switch it on like the electric light."

I imagine that astral travel would be taught when they're doing Lore. Certain things are taught to them then that are still very secretive and very deep, deep in their culture. No matter how long you live with Indigenous people you would never understand fully what's in their mind. Thousands of years of genetics. They are certainly a chosen people. They do understand the land. They can read the land better than anyone I know. They still share and practice their knowledge in Western Australia.

Trina's Dead Baby

Approximately two years after her encounter with the Christian mob, Trina was pregnant for the fifth time. Late one night she knocked on my home door saying she thought she was in labour and needed to use the toilet.

While Trina was in the loo, I ran back to my bedroom and woke my companion. I said that her baby would be arriving soon and I needed his help. "Can you go down to the clinic and get some things for me?" I asked.

"No!" he said, "If someone is having a baby, I'm going home."

"No! I need you to help!" I insisted in a whisper.

"I'm no good at anything like this!" he argued in a similar hushed tone.

"You've *got* to go to the clinic and get the things I need to deliver!" I commanded softly. I needed gloves, clean sheets, a blade to cut the cord, and something to tie it.

"I'll never be able to find these things!" he insisted.

"There is a trolley and a silver box -" I started to explain.

"I don't know what a trolley is. Do you want me to get a stretcher?" he asked.

"Go to the clinic and use your common sense! It will all be there in front of you!" I persisted.

I handed him the keys to the clinic and within a flash he returned with a handful of bandages. Bandages!! No gloves, no instruments, no sheets! He was clearly out of his element!

"I'm no good at this!" he repeated defensively. "You don't understand. I can't do this! I can't help you!" and with that, he went out the back door and drove away!

As though on cue, Trina came out of the bathroom and asked me to go and look in the toilet. When I went in there, I saw the most beautifully formed baby boy in the toilet bowl. He was cyanosed and his colouring was purple. I lifted him out knowing he was dead. The cord had been cut. All I could think about was Trina's well-being as the placenta was still inside her. I wrapped the stillborn baby in a towel. Then I asked Trina to lie down and we waited for the expulsion of the placenta.

Trina told me that she couldn't look at the baby as she knew it was dead. She asked me what sex the baby was, and I told her that it was a boy. It was 5am when I asked Trina to stay with me for a while until I knew that she would be well enough to go back to the camp.

I then took the baby to the clinic. I emptied all the drugs out of the clinic's drug fridge and put the stillborn baby in there because of the searingly hot summer weather and the fact that the nearest undertaker was over 320 kilometres away. I knew that the RFDS was due to fly in to Nullagine in three hours' time. The doctor would certify the death of the baby and do a post-natal check on Trina.

Staying Alive

Lily woke me about midnight. "Terrible fight! Come and stop them!" I quickly got into the truck. Lily was already sitting in the front seat, ready to go with me to the reserve. On arrival, I saw several small fires. A lot of noise - shouting, screaming. Beer cans flying through the air.

My attention was mainly on the children who were gleefully running around. They were lighting old clothes and throwing fireballs into the air! They seemed oblivious to the adults' fight. The children were laughing and having a good time - ducking and diving to the left and right as they missed the fire rags and some sticks that they had also thrown. The fires were raining down very close to them. They waved and called my name, pointing at the next fire object to fall. They were laughing, enjoying their new game.

My eyes went quickly to someone who had raised a small shovel above his head and he brought it down on Nancy's head. She collapsed in a heap! A stone flew by me and hit Robert on the side of the head. Other adults were punching each other, falling down in the dust. Everyone was in this big brawl! What Lily said was true: "They will kill each other!"

I went over to a blind man. He was a big and strong fella, whom I thought was the most disadvantaged. I called his name, telling him who I was. I placed my hand on his shoulder when suddenly Robert's loyal dog came from nowhere and savagely bit me. Without looking I knew the dog had torn open the back of my leg!

Any desire to help anyone left me; self-preservation dictated. I was no match for this fight! I jumped into my vehicle and took off. Arriving home, I went directly to the bathtub, turned it on, and returned with a big cup of salt. I pulled my clothes off and sat in the tub. The bath water turned into blood. I had no idea what damage had been done. I could not see it. I told myself a good bleed will wash out the germs!

There was a loud bang on the door. "Police here. There has been a big fight at the reserve. We need you."

"Go away!" I called back.

"One of them looks like he's bleeding to death!" they persisted.

"I'm in the bath. A dog has bitten me. You will have to come in and stop my bleeding. I feel like I can't walk! I need help to get out of the tub."

"Are you sure you want us to come in?"

"Absolutely."

The two men helped me out. They bandaged my leg saying, "It looks bad. It's really ripped open! Looks serious!"

I needed assistance to hop to the police truck. I was cranky. I told them I didn't want to go back to the reserve. They assured me that they had moved the injured people and had placed them on the clinic's veranda.

The police helped me out of their van and I hopped my way into the clinic. The police left. (They probably went back to the reserve to put out the fires and to investigate the incident). I had six patients to deal with. One had a small artery spurting blood from his head. I stopped the bleeding. As I was stitching his head, Anthony came in with a snake and started to poke it at my patient's face! Laughing and teasing him. I assumed it was a tree snake because the joker showed no fear. The last thing I needed to deal with was a drunk prankster!

Then I noticed the *Mabin Man* was badly injured. A lit firestick had been shoved into his nose! He was in *bad* shape. I phoned the RFDS but couldn't reach them. So, I called the closest hospital and explained that I had six patients, two seriously injured and that I wasn't able to reach the Flying Doctors.

"Nurse, you sound hysterical. You need to calm down," the on-call doctor advised.

I answered, "A dog has ripped the back of my leg open and it's hurting me. I'm in pain. And I need advice about the man's burnt nose. It's very severe!"

He answered, "Hang up. Take a deep breath and go outside. You'll feel better. I'm not in a position to help you. You're on your own." In an apparent effort to console me, he added, "It happens to me in emergency. You just have to work through it slowly, one by one."

That's fine for him, I thought. He at least has the right equipment and staff to help him. I didn't feel consoled. Nor did I hop outside. I treated each patient to the best of my ability. And when I was finished, I rang the police for a ride home. The next day the Flying Doctors came and took the *Mabin Man*, who was the only one willing to go, to the Hedland Hospital.

A couple of weeks later, I received a letter from a surgeon at Perth Hospital saying that the *Mabin Man* should have been sent directly to them - not Hedland. "We know the results would have been much better," he wrote. That wasn't my decision! The letter was tactfully written, but the tactful reprimand still stung.

When I next saw the RFD, I expressed my frustration - as though it was *my* fault that the *Mabin Man* didn't get to Perth sooner! In my heart, I am sure that if it had been a whitefella, he would have gone to their Burns Unit that very day.

"Forget it. Don't think about it," the Flying Doctor replied. "It's too late now, so just forget about it."

As much as I didn't like that advice, I knew that there were times when it was all we could do. I've often had to push things out of my mind in order to cope. It's either that or suffer severe PTSD.

A Personal Thanks to the RFDS

Words cannot express my admiration and appreciation for the Royal Flying Doctor Service. In my fifteen years working as a remote-area nurse in the Pilbara, I worked with about eight different Flying Doctors - all unique characters and experienced medicos. They were knowledgeable professionals who took good care of their patients. On a personal level, each was kind, generous, thoughtful, and tolerant.

Many people have written about the RFDS, but I want to pause a minute to acknowledge their pilot. There were so many times he risked his own life so that we could save others. Landing in Nullagine's scrublands was no small feat. The bush airport was nothing more than an unsealed airstrip. There was no control tower, and there was no one to clear the field when wild brumbies [horses] roamed about. In bad weather, dust storms would ruin the airfield and often the plane could not land due to wind erosion. Imagine the stress of knowing someone's life was hanging in the balance!

At night, kerosine drum lamps had to be placed along the runway to guide the aircraft. The police and/or I would park at the end of the runway and used the high beams on our vehicles to assist the pilot. However, we had to keep the lights off until we heard the noise of the plane and saw the flicker of its red lights. Insects were a huge problem for us. They were attracted to the light and they would hit us in the face. Great big grasshoppers would go into our hair and down the back of our shirts; big moths would hit our eyes. Gross!

Whether it was day or night, the facilities were rudimentary, to say the least! Next to the airstrip, there was a small tin shed. I had donated an old iron bed so that patients could wait more comfortably for the RFDS to arrive. There was also a pit toilet. However, a venomous red-bellied black snake lived in it so people went outside, rather than inside. In all, the area was so rugged that some of the young nurses (who accompanied the Flying

Doctors during their regular fortnightly clinics) wanted to remain on the plane because they found the remoteness so daunting. Of course, the extreme heat would make this impossible so they would reluctantly disembark.

Over the years, the pilot and doctors became my friends. They were my support system. Being on my own and in such a remote area, their acts of kindness made a big difference. They would bring me special teas, fresh buns and books. One doctor noticed I was always losing my keys so he bought me a leather belt, which he saw at a market, so I could hang my keys on it. How thoughtful! Doctors also invited me (and the police) to their family's Christmas dinner in Port Hedland. Once I even received fresh flowers - what a treat!

One of the Flying Doctors played in a band. On one occasion she asked me how I controlled my own anxiety while waiting for help to arrive. I described how I would use Tibetan chanting ("Om") to still my mind as I transported severely injured patients (a foot hanging off, for example) to the airstrip. She used our conversation to compose a song about me! It was recorded but, alas, I don't have a copy.

I hope these stories help people to realise that the RFDS is much, much more than an air-ambulance service. I could not have survived working in the Outback without them. They listened when I called out of frustration. And they gave clear directions on how to handle difficult situations. I could always count on them. They were my strength, my friends, my saviours, my blessings. As many others have said, "Thank God for the Flying Doctors".

Breakthrough

Years after the police saved her life, Cathy came back to Nullagine yet again. Obviously, she was *deeply* in love with Jason. She came to see me and said, "I feel we could change him. There's things inside him that he just can't get out. So I thought that every Sunday afternoon when you're not at work, we'd come up [to my home rather than the clinic] and sit down and have a cup of tea, and you try and talk to him."

Considering our last encounter, when Jason choked me, you might start to wonder about *me*! Living out in the desert for such a long time, there was no sequence of where people went, why they went, were they in jail, have they gone south? I never knew. People just turned up in my life and they would carry on as though they had seen me yesterday. That was just the way it was. And I found that very easy to do.

And yes, I know how foolish women can be - thinking they can change another person. Nevertheless, I said, "Oh, yeah, that's alright." I knew they had no idea of time. And, sure enough, they came at various times. Maybe 4 o'clock, maybe 2 o'clock. But that is beside the point because when they came, I'd make the tea and I would talk with Cathy. Jason would just sit there and say *nothing*. No matter how many times I included him in our conversation, he never spoke. Week after week.

On the fourth Sunday, I said to Jason, "I work very hard, and you can't keep coming up here when I want to lay down and have a sleep and you're not going to partake in this therapy. You understand what therapy means?" I asked. "Cathy believes she can make you better if you tell what makes you so angry." I continued by explaining, "What inside your heart has caused you to have this anger over the years, and it's built up?"

I sat there in silence and watched the clock tick by - three minutes, four minutes, five minutes. Then he said, "When I was a little boy, I'd come home and there was never any tucker for me. My mother said, 'You want to stay out late? Well, you don't get fed.'"

Then there was this tremendous silence again. Cathy seemed to feel that this was the revelation of all wisdom and she started to cry. She got up and hugged him, and said, "Ah, that would make anyone angry. And you carried that in your heart!" She hugged him again and kissed him and then she sat back down, sobbing.

Then Jason said, "It wasn't just *once*. It was *all* the time! In the night time, she'd never, ever save me any food. If she had food, she'd hide it. It happened for *years*! She wouldn't feed me at night."

What's the truth? Or why did this happen? How misbehaving was he as a young boy? I don't know. But Cathy and Jason saw it as the biggest breakthrough in all psychiatric therapy that you could imagine. They got up and we all hugged each other. They left and they never came back on a Sunday again.

Jason *did* change his life. They moved to Jigalong, where there was no alcohol. I saw him a couple of years later when I broke down on the road. I had a puncture. He was with a whole lot of Aboriginal men that I didn't know. He made them stop and come over. They lifted the whole truck up and (no exaggeration) in three minutes they had the bad tyre off and the good trye put on. I was so grateful! I would have missed the one and only plane that night. Jason looked steadily at me and said, "I would do anything for you, Philla."

Invitation to a Corroboree

I was leaving my clinic one afternoon when a group of young fellows called out to me, "You come down to the reserve tonight before dark. And take us out of town for a corroboree."

"What's that all about?" I asked.

"We have to show you how we dance and sing. You haven't seen that."

When I got to the reserve, there were about ten women and as many men. They climbed into my truck and we drove about 12 kilometres out of town to a special location. By the time we arrived, it was dark and a big fire was going already. I was directed to sit with the women. I could hear a didgeridoo and was shocked to see an Aboriginal man playing a rusty exhaust pipe from an old car or truck! It was incredible to hear how well he could play this!

"What special occasion is this?" I asked my companions.

They laughed loudly and explained, "We're doing this for you!"

The men had disappeared earlier and when they reappeared, they wore blue jeans but were shirtless. They were coated in white powder and waved small gum-tree branches. The women spontaneously started to clap, tap rocks together and chant. Others clicked sticks together, all to a very unusual, hypnotic beat. The dancers stamped their feet in the dust, opening and closing their legs, knocking their knees together, much like dancing the Charleston. They lifted their legs very high, as though to imitate emus and they called out animal noises. There was no alcohol, and everyone was so happy and spontaneous. Each dance was short and repeated often. After a couple of hours, we went back home. I thought to myself, this is how these people were before Captain Cook arrived.

Epilogue

During my first 10 years of living in Nullagine, I expected that I would end my days there. I had even bought a small house. When I retired, I imagined becoming an off-sider: I would help the nurse or when there was some big catastrophe, I could just help out now and again.

By 1996, which marked my 15th year of nursing in the Pilbara, I was exhausted. Burned out. Unimaginably tired. I was due for holidays, but I didn't believe I could recover in just three months. I was getting close to the pension age so I thought very seriously about not coming back. The more I thought about leaving permanently, the more appealing this notion became. I would say to myself, 'As you get older the heat will get to you', and I kept thinking about how tired and drained I felt.

One day a woman came into the clinic and I said to her just casually, "Would you like to buy my house?"

"Ah, yes… Yes!" She jumped at the opportunity. Her partner worked with the gold and there were not many houses available in the area. She named a price and I said I would sell. "It might take me a few months before I get the money ready," she said.

"That's alright. I'm going on leave in December. I'm going on holidays," I replied. And that was it. The time had come. I was too old and too worn out to go on. The stories in this book represent events I am willing to remember, let alone talk about. The Flying Doctor's advice, "Don't think about it," has served me well over the years. It has helped me to avoid the ravages of post-traumatic stress.

I never said anything to anyone about the sale, and for some reason, the buyer never mentioned it either. There was never any secrecy about it. But as I was preparing to leave, I decided simply to say that I was due to go on holidays. For a long time after I left, the Indigenous folks would say, "She will come back." Even a couple of years afterwards they predicted, "She'll come back to us. She'll come back."

Detachment is something I learned long ago. We certainly learned it in the convent and it was certainly reinforced when I went to the Buddhists (where it seemed to make more sense). If we had a letter from home we would more or less rip it up and destroy it. We never kept anything. I can honestly say that the habit of detachment is well and truly in me now. If you're not attached to material things or even people, you don't experience that great sense of loss or sadness like other people go into.

The Indigenous always insisted that I would return, while I always said that I would *never* go back. Now, as I review these stories, these memories, I realise that we both were wrong. An important part of me never really left.

The End

Acknowledgements

We would like to express our gratitude and appreciation to the following people: Debbie Clarke for her help with recording the outline of several of these stories; Patrick McGowan for sharing his experiences and advice on getting published; Annie Whybourne for her encouragement and Dominyc Barsley for his efforts at organising the initial stories into book form.

A special thanks to Gloria Chalvien and Judith Poole for their careful review and editing of this entire manuscript, to Jeff Nykiel for his insightful comments and strong encouragement, and to Dr Dorothy Pawluch who helped us to recognise and articulate the historical and cultural value these stories have to offer. We appreciate comments by Eva Nykiel who highlighted the need for an overview. Finally, to someone we called Pat (another person who values anonymity) who provided valuable background information about Nullagine and its remote lifestyle.

Suggested Readings

Cunneen, C. *Conflict, Politics and Crime: Aboriginal communities and the police.* Allen & Unwin Pty Ltd, Melbourne: 2009. Libby Book, EPUB (DRM)

Jarrett, S. *Liberating Aboriginal people from violence.* Connor Cout Publishing Pty Ltd, Brisbane: 2013.

Langford, S. *The Leading Edge. Innovation, technology and people in Australia's Royal Flying Doctor Service.* The University of Western Australia Press, Crawley, 2015.

Aboriginal and Torres Straight Islander Social Justice: *First nations women to take leading role in addressing family and community violence.* Tuesday 13 September 2022. https://humanrights.gov.au/about/news/media-releases/first-nations-women-take-leading-role-addressing-family-and-community.

About the Authors

In her mid-teens and inspired by stories of missionary work in Africa, **Philomena** joined the Sisters of Mercy in New South Wales. For 20 years she was cut off from the world as she laboured in an orphanage doing laundry. Longing to do something more meaningful, she left convent life to study and practice nursing in geriatrics, psychiatry (working with the criminally insane), and maternity. Later she volunteered overseas, using her nursing skills in Bangladesh and Calcutta.

Purely by chance, which is where these stories begin, Philomena journeyed to a Tibetan Monastery in Nepal and decided to work with the poorest and most neglected people in her own country, Australia. Her spiritual quest led her to the Pilbara, to a small mining town and an Aboriginal community where she lived and cared for the "true desert people".

For an incredible 15 years (1981-1996) Philomena remained in this remote setting. Her stories bear witness to the ravages of racism and to the fortitude of Australia's Indigenous people.

Since her retirement, she has continued her life of service by visiting prisoners, the sick, the elderly, and volunteering within the Catholic church.

Marjorie MacKinnon, PhD, is a retired academic. She worked in universities in Canada, Hong Kong and Australia. She met Philomena playing bridge on the Sunshine Coast in Queensland, Australia.

Milton Keynes UK
Ingram Content Group UK Ltd.
UKHW041014220524
443072UK00001B/42

9 780645 969108